JOURNEY

Reminders from A Guardian Angel

Memoir

Annette Forster

AuthorHouse™ UK Ltd.
500 Avebury Boulevard
Central Milton Keynes, MK9 2BE
www.authorhouse.co.uk
Phone: 08001974150

© 2011 Annette Forster. All rights reserved.

No part of this book may be reproduced, stored in a retrieval system, or transmitted by any means without the written permission of the author.

First published by AuthorHouse 2/5/2011

ISBN: 978-1-4520-7923-3 (sc)

This book is printed on acid-free paper.

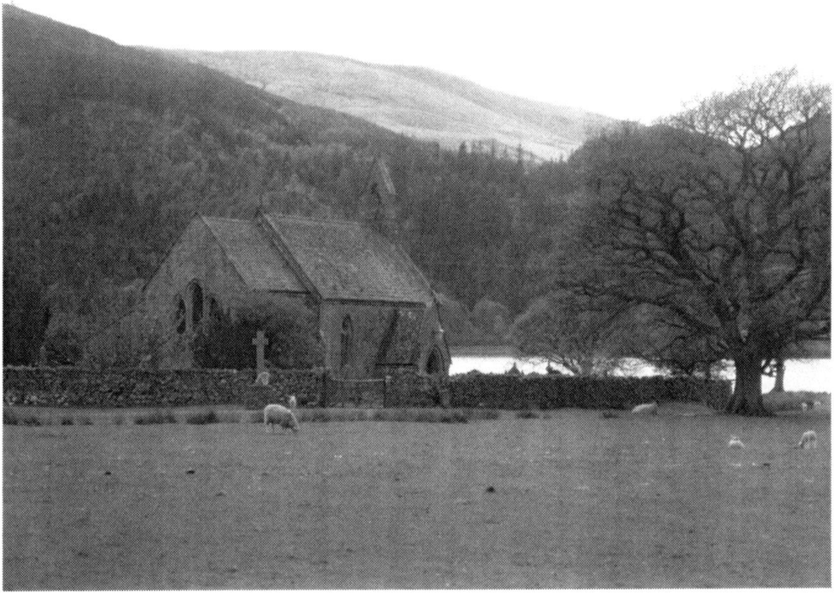

**For Lukas & Lilly, my greatest achievements
Some pointers for your journey...
And for Rob, my true love**

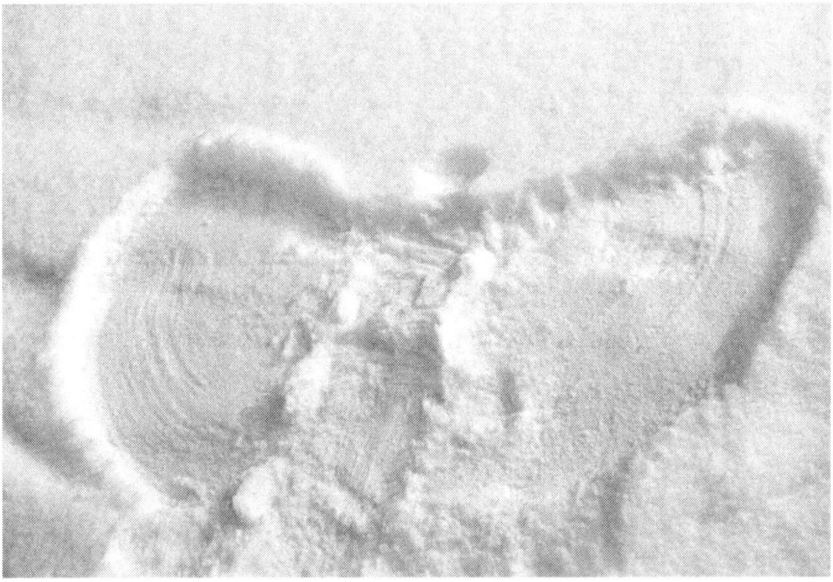

Contents

Chapter # 1.   BEING   1

Chapter # 2.   LEARNING   13

Chapter # 3.   TRAVELLING   31

Chapter # 4.   EXPERIENCING   45

Chapter # 5.   SEARCHING   59

Chapter # 6.   BELIEVING   71

Chapter # 7.   LOVING   81

Chapter # 8.   CREATING   95

Chapter # 9.   IMPROVING YOUR LEVEL OF BEING   107

Chapter # 10. ANTICIPATING   119

References and Acknowledgements: 128

Being

Chapter 1:

BEING

Being

> "We cannot obtain heavenly bliss through our strength alone, but with the assistance of divine grace; and man, despite all his follies and errors, being led by a higher hand, reaches some happy goal at last."
>
> — J.W. VON GOETHE

My name is Raphael and I have been a guardian angel and a messenger of God for what can only be described in a time designation as everlasting. When a child is created, he or she is assigned a guardian angel to protect and look after them. We, as guardian angels, can guide and influence the destiny of our charge by giving them messages which they in turn then perceive as a "gut feeling" or instinct about something. A guardian angel will stay with his charge until death. We can apply superhuman strength, if God commands it, and at times we do, but mostly we are mere messengers, inspiring thoughts and action. At times we have to stand back as our charge work things out for themselves. Sometimes bad things happen to good people, angels cannot always prevent this from happening. The reason for this is that angels cannot interfere with the free will of mankind. We cannot interfere with the free will of our own charge or that of others which will impact them. Sometimes we are there to provide comfort when suffering is inevitable. We are also there to inspire, comfort, protect and guide.

> ***Hebrews 1:14 "All the angels are spirits who serve God and are sent to help those who will receive salvation."***

Most guardian angels call our charges our children. On their journey through life we want poets, musicians, artists, writers and philosophers to inspire them. We want them to experience many episodes and events so that they can learn and grow. We inspire movies and especially music to give guidance and make the journey more enjoyable. Some humans are much more perceptive than others. Some can actually see us and talk to us. Some only see us when they are very ill or in desperate need of protection. Some can sense that we are there. Most will look back at the coincidences in their lives and wonder if something else was involved in providing some level of protection or comfort that came at just the right time.

> ***Psalm 91:11 "He has put his angels in charge of you to watch over you wherever you go."***

Angels are available to all humankind; it does not depend on someone's "worthiness". Some people choose to be more perceptive to our messages than others. Some have closed their hearts and minds to us and prefer to go it alone. We never seek to actively make contact with our charges. We care for them, protect them and guide them on behalf of God who commands us. We are anxious to hear and carry out God's Word. Our love for God motivates us to protect and guard what is most precious to Him, His children. We want our children to have a relationship with God, not with us. We move at the speed of light to carry out God's will, and we can get involved in the political affairs of nations or the smallest concerns of children.

> ***Colossians 2:18 "Do not let anyone disqualify you by making you humiliate yourself and worship angels. Such people enter into visions, which fill them with foolish pride because of their human way of thinking."***

I mostly function in a spiritual state, but in my physical state in heaven I am approximately two meters tall. I have supernatural power and am blessed with magnificent beauty. My skin sparkles like gold dust and I glow as though the sun is shining on me at sunset in the warmest of colours. My wings are soft to the touch and brilliant white. We are immortal and invisible, however we can take on the guise of humans or show ourselves to humans, if God commands it. We are exalted, high above the sinful desires of humankind.

> ***Revelation 22:8-9 "...I bowed down to worship at the feet of the angel who showed these things to me. But the angel said to me, "Do not worship me! I am a servant like you...Worship God!"***

In unseen and unknown ways to humans, we bring God's spiritual realm to the physical world. Mankind is so easily discouraged and fearful. If only God would open their spiritual eyes and enlighten their minds to understand his might and power the world would be a much better place.

In the sixties, I became the guardian angel of a girl born in Pretoria, South Africa. I call her Blue-Eyes and from an early age her emotions frequently found their way into poems. I will relay some episodes from her journey as well as give some reminders from those who achieved a higher level of being. As a messenger, I hope this will inspire and guide others as a result of the lessons learnt.

Guardian angels have been given to mankind as messengers, the word "Angel" means "messenger" in Hebrew and Greek. We have personalities which in turn influence our children in different ways. I believe I have an extra sparkle in my eye and I like to dance around to what I call a "rock-out" tune. I don't like stereotypes. I don't like boundaries and who said a tall, giant guardian angel could not dance to a great rock-out tune?

Being

As messenger, I love poetry and I love music. It creates emotions or reminds humanity of sad or enjoyable experiences, and it can conjure up a mood or create an atmosphere. Music provides the soundtrack to individual lives. Great songs are poetry that comes to life through music.

I have always been fascinated by the importance humanity places on their birth information i.e. when and where people are born, who their birth parents are and what their social standing is. Prior to having made any choices or even having the chance to develop their own viewpoints and personalities, they are often categorised by this information. They celebrate their birthdays and allocate birth signs in the East and the West. This includes information regarding the exact position of the sun and moon and all the planets at the time of birth.

Blue-Eyes was born in the sixties, famously the age of youth and change. The changes affected education, values, lifestyles, laws and entertainment. Change seems to have been the one constant in her life, she had to learn to embrace it and grow with it.

Blue-Eyes was born in South Africa – the rainbow nation. In those days, however, it was pretty black and white. She was born in Pretoria. Marthinus, son of Andries Pretorius the Boer statesman after whom the city was named, founded Pretoria in 1855. It became the capital of the Transvaal in 1869, administrative capital of South Africa in 1910 and a city in 1931.

Pretoria is famous for its lovely old buildings and wide streets, lined with Jacaranda trees. These bloom every October and November, turning the city into a purple spectacle with the streets carpeted with purple blossoms. More than 50 000 Jacaranda trees line the streets of Pretoria which is why it became known as the "Jacaranda city".

Pretoria is said to offer one of the world's best climates with warm and wind-free summers and crisp and clear winters. The climate is neither humid, nor too hot, and summer thunderstorms produce flashes of lightning and brief torrential downpours that are soon over with the sun appearing again. When Blue-Eyes was scared of the thunder, I used to tell her that it is God's way of letting people know that it was going to rain. The smell of the rain hitting the African soil is unique and filled with promises of life.

From Kenya to South Africa, the soil in Africa is red. This is because the ground is enriched with iron and aluminium that has developed over long periods of time by heavy rain falls and the intense heat. The iron is the origin of the redness, but according to folklore the red soil of Africa is from all the blood that has been spilled there. Then there are the stars which somehow appear closer to Earth from the southern hemisphere. The most distinctive is the Southern Cross, also known as Crux, which is made up of five very bright stars which together form the shape of a cross. The Southern Cross points to the south. Several countries in the southern hemisphere have used this distinctive symbol of the night skies. For example Brazil depicted it on postage stamps, it appears on the Coat of Arms of the Commonwealth of Australia, and in South Africa a prestigious award is the Honoris Crux Decoration for bravery.

As a child, Blue-Eyes grew up with a swimming pool and a trampoline and a tree house that her dad made for them. She didn't realise how fortunate she was growing up in the sunshine with nature around her and with the freedom of so much space. I had to warn her to take care not to step on snakes or scorpions. She was taught always to lift the rocks up away from her and only to eat fruit and vegetables that were eaten by the birds or animals. One of Blue-Eyes' friends at age six ate wild mushrooms because she would not listen to her guardian angel and she got very ill and passed away. Sometimes, someone is visited by the Angel of Death and when this happens, there is not much that we can do. At other times, we can make miracles happen to keep our children safe, when the Angel of Death is not around.

Despite being the most economically advanced country on the African continent, South Africa was among the last countries in Africa to introduce television broadcasting to its population. The main reason was that television was suspected to undermine the apartheid government's ideology. They also saw television as a threat to Afrikaans, giving undue prominence to English and creating unfair competition for the Afrikaans' press. Prime Minister Hendrik Verwoerd compared television with atom bombs, claiming that "they are modern things, but that does not mean they are desirable. The government has to watch for any dangers to the people, both spiritual and physical". The Dutch Reformed Church also proclaimed it at the time as the "devil's own box, for disseminating communism and immorality".

Remember that God's greatest gift to mankind is free will, and even in Church this free will can sometimes lead to views or rules that are not from God. Many South Africans, including Afrikaners, did not share these views and when Neil Armstrong landed on the moon in 1969, South Africa was one of the few countries unable to watch the event live. Finally in 1975, experimental broadcasts began in the main cities before a nationwide service commenced on January 1976 when Blue-Eyes was seven years old. Growing up with no television and no computers meant that Blue-Eyes and her friends and siblings played outside in the fresh air and read books for entertainment. Today, children in the Western world have TV's and computers and if they learn to balance these great sources of information and entertainment with playing in the fresh air and reading books, they are so blessed. There are still countries in the world controlling their media and nothing in life should be taken for granted.

Blue-Eyes played Cinderella in her school play. She couldn't sing, so the choir had to fill in for her singing parts. She "married" the prince at the age of twelve and as she stood there in her beautiful gown with the prince on his knees, she wondered who her real prince was going to be. Like all little girls, all she wanted was a fairy-tale life and a handsome prince to arrive on a starry night...

One of our main tasks as guardian angels is to help our children find their partner in life but more about that later.

At the age of twelve, Blue-Eyes' parents got divorced. This brought its share of pain and disillusionment to her and her family. She did not understand all the complicated issues surrounding such a painful event at the time, and she chose to be put in a boarding school. I was very close to her at this time. Life will knock you down and these knocks are what form your character. The knocks are not important, but what is important is how you get up from them and what you learn from them. You can choose to be a victim or you can choose to be a stronger person.

Where one was born and how you grew up and where you went to school is only relevant in that it contributes to one's *being*. BEING is the expression of who you are. I always remind my children of the importance of their *being* and how to improve their level of *being*.

Although it is important to know who you are, it is just as important to respect others and the fact that their *being* may be different to yours. It is important to have tolerance, understanding and humility.

Just as cream will always rise to the top, so will certain individuals regardless of their background, education or birth information.

Some individuals have managed to improve their level of being. I have repeated their thoughts as quotations to help inspire Blue-Eyes and others to express themselves creatively and to improve their level of being:

> *"Remember that you are an actor in a drama of such sort as the author chooses. If short, then in a short one. If long, then in a long one. If it be his pleasure that you should enact a poor man, see that you act it well; or a cripple, or a ruler, or a private citizen. For this is your business, to act well a given part; but to select it belongs to another." Epictetus – The Enchiridion.*

> *"You can understand other people only as much as you understand yourself and only on the level of your own being." P.D. Ouspensky –The Psychology of Man's Possible Evolution.*

> *"To be, or not to be: that is the question." William Shakespeare – Hamlet.*

BEING

The expression of who you are
Our level of consciousness
Being

Ability to live
Not only exist
Seeing

Through life experiences
Create will and understanding
The process of evolution

Never accepting average
Choose to be demanding
Start a revolution

If run out of town
Turn around
Then lead the crowd

Stop focusing on trying to get what you want
Try to know who you are

Lift your level of consciousness
Reach for the stars

So much beauty around us
In our unchosen fate
Accept every blessing

Let awareness surround us
These thoughts permeate
A higher level of Being

Learning

Chapter 2:
LEARNING

"I want to beseech you...to be patient toward all that is unsolved in your heart and to try to love the questions themselves like locked rooms and like books that are written in a very foreign tongue. Do not now seek the answers, which cannot be given you because you would not be able to live them. And the point is, to live everything. Live the questions now. Perhaps you will then gradually, without noticing it, evolve some distant day into the answer." Rainier Maria Rilke – Letters to a Young Poet. Translated by M.D Herter Norton.

Guardian angels are wise in that we have learnt from our own experiences and we have witnessed the existence of humanity for centuries. We take guidance from God and we learn from our children and know them better than anyone else. We know their thoughts, their dreams and ambitions. We know what scares them and how to influence and protect them. In their journeys through life we try to teach them and guide them.

Angels are the most powerful beings in the universe: intelligent and with free will, although we are not gods. We continually worship the one, true Creator of the Universe and execute his authority in heaven and on Earth. We are to be respected, not worshipped as immensely powerful, supernatural beings. We are there to guard, help, protect, strengthen and inspire, and we are witnesses to the lives of our charges.

Blue-Eyes went to a small school in the middle of nowhere and was picked up by the school bus which travelled for thirty minutes on a dirt road to get there. She and her friends had to chase the cows from the fields before doing sports and the ducks off the swimming pool before swimming lessons. She can vaguely remember some politically incorrect speeches she heard in school as a child in South Africa in the seventies. Although the children were told not to question the government or the Church, there was a wave of questioning and unease which started with their parents

Learning

and which gained momentum with Blue-Eyes' generation in the eighties and nineties.

It was part of my role as guardian angel to help Blue-Eyes understand that it is important to respect your elders but always make up your own mind. Question, challenge and make considered responses in life.

Although Blue-Eyes went to a small primary school, it was a loving and nurturing environment that gave her confidence and courage for later life. It is not the amount of school fees that shape a child's life, but an environment of respect, love, discipline and encouragement that will make a difference.

Every year, on spring day, which was early September in South Africa, the children would wear beautiful sun dresses to school with flowers in their hair and they would usually choose a spring king and queen. On their birthdays they would pin flowers to the birthday girl, (the boys thought this was uncool) and Blue-Eyes' most vivid memories of her childhood are the smell of fragrant flowers on hot sunny days and the smell of the earth after a thunder storm.

At high school in the eighties, Blue-Eyes encountered the struggle to be cool. She went to a high school in Pretoria which happened to be one of the largest schools in the country. I guess the problem was that her interpretation of cool was not exactly the same as that of the in-crowd. In this struggle for coolness she wore plastic earrings, jelly shoes and massive shoulder pads. She had a perm and HUGE hair, all of which I tried my best to warn her against! I told her to concentrate on learning, doing as many extracurricular activities as possible, and to enjoy the power and beauty of her youth.

At university she came into her own. She was constantly surrounded by interesting people and it was cool to be yourself. This period of learning was a definite highlight on Blue-Eyes' journey. She joined the debating society as well as the hiking club. She hiked all over South Africa and neighbouring countries. She learned to dive and she did skydiving and paragliding. She bungee jumped off the Bloukranz Bridge and fell 216 meters, near the beautiful town of Storms River, Cape Town. I had my hands full being her guardian angel, but I guess there is something exciting about jumping off a perfectly safe bridge with nothing but a piece of elastic to stop you from plunging into the ground below. She thought it was such an adrenaline rush that she had to do it again off the Gouritz River Bridge near Mossel Bay where she also did a pendulum swing. It was insane! She put on a harness and stepped off a bridge where she fell 65m before swinging under another bridge, squealing with delight!

Blue-Eyes river-rafted and sailed and embraced every beautiful opportunity that life presented. You have to have fun, embrace life, and grab every opportunity, but don't be reckless with your own life or anyone else's. Blue-Eyes and her friends would hollow out a water melon, and then fill it with vodka, orange juice, lemonade, vanilla ice-cream and lots of ice – delicious! Yes, she did step out of line from time to time. However she avoided the pitfalls of binge drinking and yob culture that happen to bored youths in many parts of the world.

The best lessons that Blue-Eyes learnt at University had very little to do with the content of her qualifications. Apart from having fun and the life experience, the single most important lesson she learnt was what I call "thinking skills". She learned how to study, how to remember, using certain thought processes and logical thinking.

Another lesson I told Blue-Eyes was that education is so important. What education gives, money can't buy – it gives you options in life! The more educated you are, the more options you have, the more informed choices you can make in your life.

Students think they are larger than life. Students think they will live forever and have the right to live life to the fullest. On a weekend like any other, one of Blue-Eyes' best friends stayed with her at the commune where she lived at the time. She shared a house with four housemates and they had a butler with a tuxedo. They would have "Zorba-the-Greek" parties where all their plates were smashed and then "replace-a-plate" parties where the entrance fee at the gate was a plate!

They had a barbecue outside in the sunshine and Blue-Eyes' friend's boyfriend came to pick her up in his new Porsche. They agreed to meet up in a bar that evening. At about nine pm they were talking on their mobile phones when Blue-Eyes' friend said to her, "We are doing low flying on the motorway…" and then the phone went dead. She never arrived and Blue-Eyes eventually went home. I tried to comfort Blue-Eyes as the Angel of Death came for her friend and at four am in the morning the police came to tell her that her friend had died in an accident. How does one explain shock and grief to someone who's been fortunate enough not to have experienced it? It is irrational, that much I know. Blue-Eyes sat under a table and refused to come out for hours. I sat there with her and although she did not know it, I held her close.

GOODBYE

When I close my eyes
I can see you smile
When I look up to the sky
I keep asking why?

Our arms are empty
Our hearts are full
So many things I wish I'd said
So many things I will never forget

Goodbye my friend
This is not the end
Until we meet again
Keep smiling up in heaven

I blow a kiss to the sky
For now it's goodbye
Until we meet again
Up in heaven

Learning

During her fourth year at University, Blue-Eyes got elected Miss Intervarsity. This was a bit of a poster girl title and certainly not her claim to fame, but it got her involved in charity work. She got to represent the University of Pretoria (TUKS) at various events, she got to meet famous people and it was another fun, growth experience.

One of Blue-Eyes' favourite projects was to teach kids from children's homes what I call life-ability skills. Literacy aside, these kids did not know how to open a bank account, how to write a CV or resume, how to conduct a job interview or, basically, how to manage their lives. Many individuals don't always realise how much they are taking for granted and how much they have to give to society. Blue-Eyes' one regret on her journey so far was not having done more, and her one ambition for the future is to find a way to really make a difference.

As a student at the University of Pretoria, Blue-Eyes would hang out in Hatfield which had a thriving music scene. Reggae music was very popular, as was rock, jazz, or anything but pop, which was very un-cool at the time. Blue-Eyes loved live music, especially in her favourite bar called Bootleggers where one of her best friends always sat next to a certain pillar, as though he was part of the fixtures of the place. There was a cocktail mixer from Australia who entertained the crowds, and a saxophone player whom she dated for a year without ever knowing his surname.

South Africa, at the southern tip of the continent of Africa, is one of the most fascinating places on Earth for its geographical and cultural diversity. Its history is as colourful as the country itself. After the British seized the Cape of Good Hope area in 1806, many of the Dutch settlers (the Boers) trekked north to find their own territory. Many Boer traditions, such as eating "beskuit" or "rusks" which you dip in your coffee and "biltong" which is dried beef jerky, still exist today. The Boers used these methods to preserve their food in trekking up North with their ox wagons. South Africa gained independence from the UK on 31 May, 1910. The discovery of diamonds (1867) and gold (1886) spurred wealth and immigration and increased the subjugation of the natives.

The political climate was changing with massive debates, although Blue-Eyes did not realise the scope of changes and historical importance of what she was witnessing at the time.

In 1985 during PW Botha's infamous "Rubicon" speech, in which the then South African president refused to countenance any move towards democracy and where he wagged his finger in anger, Blue-Eyes thought to herself that the situation was hopeless and I comforted her that there is always hope.

Blue-Eyes did not see any live music concerts whilst growing up, as everyone boycotted South Africa. She grew up with economic and cultural sanctions imposed upon South Africa and she felt like she was left behind in terms of the development and excitement happening in the rest of the world. This is another thing so often taken for granted in countries frequented by pop and rock stars: the freedom to hold concerts and the freedom to attend.

Once when Blue-Eyes was fifteen years old the rock group Queen, performed at Sun City in South Africa. Sun City is in one of the former homelands called Bophuthatswana which was one of ten territories assigned to the black majority population in the 1950's as part of the South African government's policy of apartheid, or racial segregation. So it meant that the concert was not officially in South Africa even though it was within a few hours' drive of Johannesburg. Blue-Eyes loved the Queen concert and thought that Freddie Mercury was amazing! She thought at the time that if that was the one and only concert she would ever be able to attend in her life, it would have been worth it.

The performances at Sun City were to land the band in hot water. Many well-known acts, both before and after Queen, have played at the luxurious holiday resort in the desert and were not subsequently criticized for it. However, the international outcry against apartheid reached a high-point shortly after the band performed. Many action groups, including a group of musicians called Artists United Against Apartheid, publicly condemned Queen, and some other acts, for their performances at the exclusive resort. They released a song "I ain't gonna play Sun City," which became a political anthem, a rallying cry for more sanctions. It was performed at Free Nelson Mandela concerts everywhere. On the positive side, people took a stance around the world to make a difference. On the negative side, South Africans were subjected to more economic and other sanctions that isolated the country even further.

In 1990, in his opening address to parliament, State President F.W. de Klerk announced that the ban on different political parties such as the African National Congress would be lifted and that Nelson Mandela would be released after 27 years in prison. Nelson Mandela was released on February 11th, 1990, and in March 1990, South West Africa became independent under the name Namibia. In May, the government began talks with the ANC. In 1991, the Acts which restricted land ownership, specifying separate living areas and classified people by race, were abolished.

Violence was increasing in the South African townships, some white right-wing groups were becoming more prominent and friends and family were arguing about the future of the country and the fear of change. A national referendum was announced for the white electorate which was meant to test the government's support. The National Party had a massive "Yes" vote campaign for change and warned white voters that a "No" vote would mean continuation of international sanctions, the danger of civil war and worsening chaos in South Africa. The "no" campaign led by Dr. Andries Treurnicht warned of "black majority rule" and "communist rule" and how the country would be doomed under either of these. The question asked in the referendum was "Do you support continuation of the reform process which the State President began on February 2, 1990, and which is aimed at a new constitution through negotiation? The results were a 69% yes vote. Of course the angels were very involved in this process. This referendum was held in 1992 and it was the last time that only "whites" voted on an issue in South Africa. For many white South Africans it sparked debates and fears of leadership and ownership much more so than about racial issues. The end of apartheid became inevitable; however, the path to the first free elections was marred by violence, killings, attacks and thousands died in township battles between the African National Congress (ANC) and the Inkata Freedom Party (IFP) again in a bid for leadership. When humankind executes free will, we have to stand by and let them.

One day Blue-Eyes was home alone with Anna, the housekeeper. Anna came running into the house hysterical and said that someone was trying to break into the house. Blue-Eyes stayed very calm. When she could hear voices she shouted that she had a gun and would not hesitate to shoot. A lot of people own firearms in South Africa. She managed to persuade the burglars that she was heavily armed and they ran away. I was standing guard at the door and I urged Blue-Eyes to stay calm.

Another time Blue-Eyes was driving and stopped at a traffic light. She always locked her doors, as I asked her to do, but she suddenly heard a loud noise. Someone had put half a tennis ball

Learning

over the lock on her car door and banged it hard, hoping the suction would open the central locking of the car so that it could be hijacked. I kept my hand on the lock and urged her to stay calm and drive off safely.

Afrikaners, of which Blue-Eyes is one, have been in Africa as long as whites in America. They are South African, they were born there and their ancestors lived there since 1652. Many white South Africans feared what would happen to their identity, their culture and their destiny because they were in such a minority. They were born in South Africa and had nowhere else to go.

It was a frightening time leading up to the first free elections. There were people camping out on the lawn in front of Blue-Eyes' family home, claiming that the property would become theirs following the election and victory by the ANC. The uneducated can easily be manipulated and misinformed.

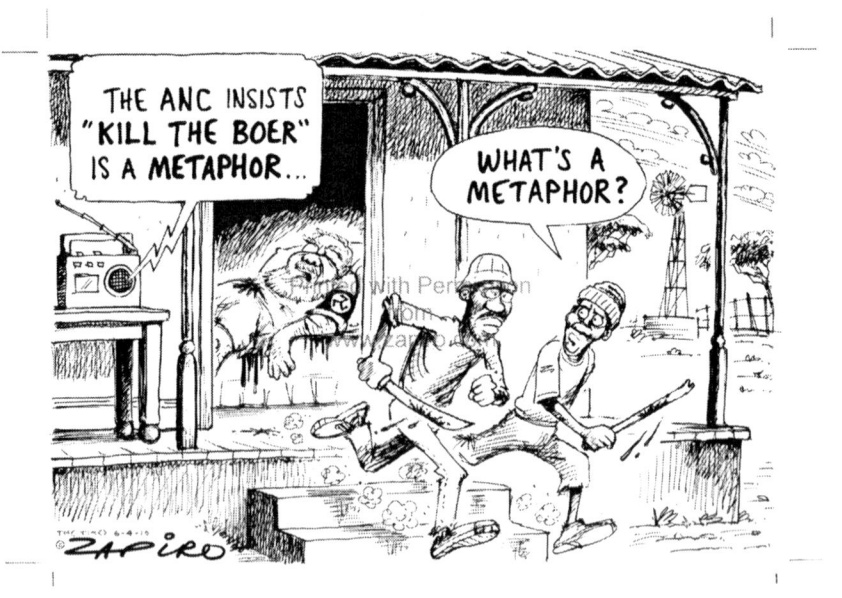

© 2010 Zapiro

Through all the challenges, the process of change moved forward and in 1994 South Africa held an election where everyone in the country could vote for the first time. Nelson Mandela was elected President.

Questions of identity and nationhood are some of the most fundamental in politics and not unique to South Africa.

Nelson Mandela wrote in *Long Walk to Freedom*, *"I think we are a shining example to the entire world of people drawn from different racial groups who have a common loyalty, a common love, to their common country."*

Although South Africa still faces many challenges today, the miracle of South Africa is that it achieved unity. In current times, it appears that Afrikaner arts, literature, cookery and rock festivals are in renaissance. South Africa is an example of binding together different nationalities, different belief systems, different values and different languages in one country. It's like Israelis and Palestinians or Protestants and Catholics forced to live together and rather than pursuing civil war, they extended hands of friendship. As angels, we work hard around the world to achieve unity.

In my role as guardian angel I want to help people understand that in order to open up for new opportunities, you have to learn to let go. Despite fear, you have to move forward with humility and understanding.

Courage does not mean being without fear, but it is moving forward in spite of it. Unity does not mean being without differences, instead it is accepting and respecting those differences.

Learning

Archbishop Desmond Tutu coined the phrase "Rainbow Nation" and South Africa is often described as a world in one country. It is truly beautiful and fascinating with all its diversity. The new republic of South Africa is divided into nine provinces and has eleven official languages. Since the ANC first came to power in 1994, an estimated 750, 000 whites have left South Africa, taking their skills with them. Roughly 4.5 million whites remain, making up 9% of the population. The main reasons that people left were the growing crime and violence as well as the growing corruption of the leadership in the country. Those who left will always have a sense of loss, as they have left their roots behind, their friends, their families and their support structures. They will of course make new friends and possibly gain new families and support structures, but if you ask any South African living abroad what they miss about South Africa, the list is very long. The beautiful climate, the laid back and down to earth attitude towards life, the fresh fruit and vegetables, the fruit juices, *rusks* and *biltong*, the smell of the earth after a thunderstorm, the calm of the wide open spaces, sitting around a fire and looking at the stars or having a "braai" barbeque with friends.

Leadership is the key to the wellbeing of a nation. Leaders however all have free will, and they choose how to lead.

I know the guardian angel of Nelson Mandela who taught him to be one of the greatest leaders of all time. Some call him a "universal conscience". Most people think that great leadership is all about talk and charisma; however, Nelson Mandela lead with kindness and humility. He was a great listener and he helped to make the miracle of South Africa happen.

Soon after the first general elections in 1994 that saw Nelson Mandela elected as President, the world opened its arms to South Africa for the first time since Blue-Eyes was born. When she reached her early twenties most performers in the world wanted to perform in South Africa. It was concert overload! Blue-Eyes and her friends would eat a triple garlic pizza before the concert and have a competition to see who could reach the front of the stage first!

One Christmas holiday as a student, Blue-Eyes went on holiday to Jeffrey's bay, better known as surfer's paradise. On New Year's Eve, they went to a party and drove back to where they were staying. She was sitting in the back of the car and when they approached the corner, I knew they were not going to make it. The wheels lifted slowly off the ground and as the car rolled, everything seemed to happen in slow motion. I wrapped myself around Blue-Eyes and she did not feel any pain, she did not think of anything other than experiencing the sounds and seeing the world go by in unnatural angles. The car stopped very close to the bedroom window of a retired couple who was sleeping inside. Fortunately, no one was badly injured, except for having cuts and bruises. Blue-Eyes closed her eyes and said "Thank You" and I winked in return. Blue-Eyes visited the retired couple later and giggled when the lady told her that her husband saw the light coming through the window, shook her arm and said: "It's time… they have come for us".

At University, Blue-Eyes met her first love. I call him that because at that age a lot of things are confused for love. Fascination, lust, intrigue, friendship…

When little girls dream of princes, no-one tells them of the amount of frogs that they will encounter during their search for a prince. Not that First Love was a frog. (They came later). First Love was really interesting, unlike anyone she had met up to that stage of her journey. He was very tall and had long hair down to his waist. The hair was definitely one of those student statements. I would be amused by people staring at him. They would literally walk into signposts looking at him. He was doing his honours degree in Economics and Blue-Eyes was in her first year at university when they met. They were together for six years. I told her they weren't meant to be together, but breaking up always hurts...

FIRST LOVE

You taught me the meaning
Of being alive
Of sharing one's feelings
And being able to cry

Since you've gone I travelled far
In search of the unknown
I learned a lot, I laughed some times
Always alone

What we shared was special
I miss it a lot
To laugh, to love, to cry, to hurt
I almost forgot

I'm in search of a soul mate
I'm tired of being alone
Everybody's got someone
They call home

I met a lot of people
I've been around
I wish I could forget
The love I once found

What went wrong?
I really don't know
Guess we had things to do
And places to go

I am reaching my dreams
I hope you are proud
Just, sometimes I wish
I could tell you out loud

Travelling

Chapter 3:
TRAVELLING

"Imagine someone living in the depths of the sea. He might think that he was living on the surface, and seeing the sun and the other heavenly bodies through the water; he might think that the sea was the sky. He might be so sluggish and feeble that he had never reached the top of the sea, never emerged and raised his head from the sea into this world of ours, and seen for himself – or even heard from someone who had seen it – how much purer and more beautiful it really is than the one in which his people live. Now we are in just the same position."
Plato – The Last Days of Socrates.

"*The ancients believed that the planets can also play notes or strike chords, creating a celestial song. Sometimes in life, the symphony of the stars and planets evoke a deeply poignant atmosphere. When you learn to follow the rhythm and appreciate the notes, high and low, you will start to appreciate life's hidden harmony.*" Jonathan Cainer

"Talking to my Angel" by Melissa Etheridge:

Don't be afraid
Close your eyes
Lay it all down
Don't you cry

Can't you see I'm going
Where I can see the sun rise
I've been talking to my angel
And he said that it's alright...

Blue-Eyes was on a hill in the Transkei. She was nineteen. It was a cloudy day and the grass was blowing in the wind. She ended a long hike up the Transkei coast that took a couple of weeks and had a sense of accomplishment when she looked at a rock called "Hole in the wall". The elements had carved a hole in this massive rock and waves were pouring through the opening. Someone put *"The Tide is Turning" by Roger Waters* on their car stereo and as the waves crushed through the rock and local children danced in

Travelling

the wind covered in beads they made out of seashells, I knew she was experiencing what I call a heavenly moment.

For Blue-Eyes, travelling is sacred. Possibly as a result of growing up in a country that was completely isolated from the rest of the world. Or it may be because the nearest flight from South Africa to anywhere takes at least ten hours. Or it could be because the exchange rate makes it so difficult for South Africans to travel abroad and visas are often required, but I guess mostly because I have taught her a sense of curiosity.

As a teenager, the song that had the biggest impact on Blue-Eyes' life and always played in her mind was *"The Ballad of Lucy Jordan" by Marianne Faithfull*. She was haunted by those words:

The Ballad of Lucy Jordan
by Marianne Faithfull:

...At the age of thirty-seven she realised she'd never
Ride through Paris in a sports car with the warm wind in her hair
So she let the phone keep ringing and she sat there softly singing
Little nursery rhymes she'd memorised in her daddy's easy chair

Her husband, he's off to work and the kids are off to school
And there are, oh, so many ways for her to spend her day
She could clean the house for hours or rearrange the flowers
Or run naked through the shady street screaming all the way...

Blue-Eyes always wanted to travel. One of my roles as guardian angel is to present prayers to God on behalf of my children. She wanted to experience the cultures, the fragrances, the differences and similarities. One night she had a dream. She dreamt she was on a beach and looking up at the sky. A cloud took the shape of a big hand that pointed across the water and a voice said: "Come, child. If you want to travel, I will show you". Blue-Eyes did not know what it meant then, but she would soon start to travel on a massive, global scale for the next twenty years with the knowledge that God wanted her to see and experience it all. She did not deserve such a gift and she often wonders why God gave it to her, but it makes me smile because the old saying is so true: Be careful what you ask for because you may just get it!

A week after the dream, Blue-Eyes resigned from her job, leaving her long-term boyfriend to go travelling on her own around the world. This was so out of character for her since she had grown up very protected and had never before even been to the pictures on her own. Of course she was not on her own, as God instructed me to show her the world and protect her. She was very scared, but knew this was something she had to do. So at the age of 23, she took a backpack and flew to Europe. She was on her own and this mobility turned out to be a great asset in her case, although I wouldn't recommend it for everyone. If you are waiting for the right time for extensive travel or for enough money or to find the right people to travel with, you will never begin the journey. It is one of those things that you just do, or else you will spend the rest of your life wishing you had done it.

On her very first flight from Johannesburg to Germany, the plane Blue-Eyes was travelling on got into difficulties. I had to work overtime and the plane managed to perform an emergency landing in Luxembourg as they were equipped to service an airplane in distress. All Blue-Eyes thought in her excitement was that she was going to get to see another country! She was not fazed by the emergency landing in a different country!

Travelling

So Blue-Eyes drove through Paris in a sports car with the warm wind in her hair...

She worked and travelled her way through Europe before moving across the Atlantic to explore the United States of America. She drove through the States on a Harley and river-rafted and bungee-jumped and hiked down the Grand Canyon. Travelling provided many heavenly moments. At times, certain places disappointed her, maybe because her expectations were too high, and other times I showed her gems that she never heard of before.

One of those gems was the Island of Mainau. This Island is fondly known as "The Flowery Isle" and consists of 40 hectares of gardens set in Lake Constance (Bodensee) on the German-Swiss border. After World War II, the grounds were kept open to the public. The little island keeps about 80 skilled gardeners fully occupied all year long.

Blue-Eyes was like a sponge, soaking up the differences and similarities she encountered on her way.

MONACO

Helicopter pilot promised paradise
A place full of compromise
Playground for the rich and famous
Doesn't pay to be Anonymous

Expectations created
As I anticipated
I had arrived
And I felt so alive!

JOURNEY

Enjoyed the Jacuzzi
Sipped some champagne
Phoned my friends
Enjoyed the vain

Gold, diamonds and pearls
Princes, stars and Earls
Different status, titles and means
Similar desires, ambitions and dreams

Looking past the royalty
Wearing off the novelty
Starting to see through different eyes
Another side of paradise

Compromise showing on young women's faces
Trying to keep in step with older men's paces
Feigning affection
Fearing rejection

The world is full of trickery
Men wearing too much jewellery
Ego's and bank balances
Hiding other inadequacies

Easy to be blinded
To what virtue there is
I found myself yearning
For silence and peace

You Live, You Learn
You experience and grow
You strive to be happy
And the richness will show

    Sometimes she met people that were real gems. One such family was from Bielefeld, Germany. Gisela was a doctor and her husband Ingo was a reporter for a local newspaper. They had a wine gallery as well as an art gallery as part of their residence. Blue-Eyes had long discussions with them over a glass of wine in their respective broken English and German. They had five adopted children from Cambodia. Ingo was a brilliant cook and believed one's sophistication was measured by the amount of herbs and spices with which one cooked. Blue-Eyes silently wondered if the salt in her cupboard at home counted. One of the first things she did on her return was to start her own herb garden. She still didn't cook, but she felt so sophisticated!

In the USA, she met another fascinating family from Boston, Massachusetts. Susan ran a successful business and was a wonderful wife and mother. She is Blue-Eyes' role model to this day. Susan's husband Richard was a carpenter and philosopher and they discussed Gibran and life in the West.

In Switzerland she lived in a house with a nuclear bunker. Switzerland passed a law at the height of the cold war in the 1960's requiring space in a nuclear fallout shelter for every resident. This means that the country has nuclear bunkers for almost every home and there is a joke that claims that following a nuclear attack, only the Swiss and cockroaches will survive!

Whilst travelling, one has a lot of time to be still, to reflect and to think. Blue-Eyes travelled alone, but never felt alone. She sensed my presence or befriended the locals or joined fellow travellers, if they headed in the same direction. Her mum and friends joined her once on a trip to Scotland. They visited the ruins of the Urquhart castle on Loch Ness and as they all sat staring at the lake, looking for Nessie or caught up in their own thoughts, her friend wrote:

A LITTLE PIECE OF PEACE [1]

Breath of a Scotsman
Filled the crisp air
With ancient music
Of days gone by

A winding path
Of grass green lawns
Encouraging me to conjour
Up images in my mind's eye

Entering the rugged ruins
Of the Urquhart Castle
Across the oblique draw bridge

A noble residence built
Cheerful chambers, rolling rooms, a charming chapel
Each positioned on their own ridge

Allowing the rare September sunlight in Scotland
To captivate me
By dancing on the mysterious Loch Nessie

The castle placed between Loch and Glen
A castle of great revere
Guards not allowing the enemy near

The bagpipes' beautiful bellowing
Fade into my reality
I found myself sitting on a stone wall
In the center chapel of this once kingly abode

---

1. Permission granted by Nicole Bekker to publish poem.

> Experiencing an overwhelming peace
> And truly knowing
> Where lay my security
>
> © Nicole Bekker

The year spent travelling in Europe and North America was merely the beginning and Blue-Eyes will be a lifelong traveller. Her travels since have included trips to Australia, New Zealand, Hong Kong, China, Singapore, Thailand, Korea, Japan, Brazil, Eastern Europe, Ireland and many other places she visited for business and pleasure.

She was once in New Zealand in the Bay of Islands on a yacht when they encountered a hurricane and she thought, what a cool way to go! Needless to say, I had to work as hard as ever to keep her safe as her journey was not yet completed.

From all her travels, the biggest lesson learnt was not the differences, but the similarities she encountered. Regardless of nationality or standing in society, everyone has very similar fears, ambitions and dreams. Some choose to pursue those ambitions and dreams, some fear change too much to step out of the comfort zone.

"Drops of Jupiter" by Train:

> *…Now that she's back from that soul vacation*
> *Tracing her way through the constellation, hey*
> *She checks out Mozart while she does Tae-Bo*
> *Reminds me that there's room to grow, hey*

Now that she's back in the atmosphere
I'm afraid that she might think of me as
Plain ol' Jane told a story about a man
Who was too afraid to fly so he never did land…

At some times during her travels she had to apply the "Coca-cola rule" you empty the contents of a bottle of coke on the outside of the room to attract all living creatures away from your bed! At other times she travelled first class and saw some of the most beautiful sights and extreme luxury this world has to offer.

The energy that allows humanity to exist is very powerful and it is a skill to be still when you are constantly moving. Wherever you can, stop for a moment and recognise what a miracle your existence is, and when you do this life seems to respond. The more gratitude you can summon, the happier you will be. Find one thing to be happy about and you will soon find ten more.

THANK YOU

Thank You for Your presence
For making a difference
In the lives touched

For us being able to travel
Learning to unravel
Differences and similarities

For providing answers
To our many questions
If only we would listen

Thank You for growth and learning
Even if we don't always understand
The plans of the Upper Hand

Experiencing

Chapter 4:
EXPERIENCING

Experiencing

"It is a permanent principle that one has to work beyond one's capacities to change one's level of being." P. D. Ouspensky, *The Psychology of Man's Possible Evolution*

Angels are messengers and guardians. Sometimes we work alone; sometimes we work in glorious groups at special times. We are often criticised that it appears as though we come to the aid of people in sometimes mundane circumstance such as a stalled car in a snowstorm, and obviously there are many people in much graver need of help. For me it is the hardest work when I cannot help. Remember, I cannot interfere with free will, I act under instruction and I respond well to prayer.

"I think prayer or some appeal from the whole heart to a force outside our circle of life which alone can alter things there, is the only possibility in certain insoluble circumstances. But surely we must cry to be shown the way out, to be shown the unseen ladder out of the impasse, and be very ready to accept whatever is shown. Then if some new idea, some new light comes into one's heart – as it will – one must be prepared to obey courageously. If one does so, one will be led out of the maze." Rodney Collin. *The Theory of Conscious Harmony.*

Traditional Catholic prayer to one's guardian angel:

Angel of God, my guardian dear
To whom God's love commits me here
Ever this day/night be at my side
To light, to guard, to rule and guide
Amen

Experiencing

As angels, we are always busy helping, guiding and inspiring, and when we see someone being inspired, someone listening or someone moving towards their destiny as a result of our actions, that is our idea of having fun.

"Business should be fun. Without fun, people are left wearing emotional raincoats most of their working lives. Building fun into business is vital; it brings life into our daily being. Fun is a powerful motive for most of our activities and should be a direct path of our livelihood. We should not relegate it to something we buy after work with money we earn." Michael Phillips. *Honest Business.*

Blue-Eyes started life in a cubicle soon after her return from her first year travelling. She had jobs in the past, but this was her first career move. With it came her first company car, budgets, forecasts, networking and all the other corporate activities which she loved and enjoyed with other like-minded people. She liked the blue-chip company she worked for which allowed her to travel even more! She was lucky. She had so much fun.

Blue-Eyes worked for a large corporation who arranged a family day every year. This was an incentive to thank employees and their families for all their hard work during the year. As she was single at the time, she did not have much fun at family day. I whispered in her ear, and she suggested to the leadership of the organisation that all employees without children should each take two children from a local orphanage on the day trip. It was agreed and became an annual event. Many children benefited who would not have had the opportunity.

At some point much later in her life, Blue-Eyes couldn't help wondering "what if" Lucy Jordan had made different choices in her life. What if Lucy Jordan chose a career instead?

THE BALLAD OF CAREER LUCY JORDAN

At the age of thirty seven
She realised, she may never have
Happy ever after as it was meant to be
A house with a tree and a family

She knew prince charming
And they could have been there
But she had her career
And he had his rock and roll affair

She met him on a Saturday night
She looked into those eyes and lost the fight
She dreamt of walking down the aisle
She surrendered to that smile

He said "Honey I'm gonna be a big star"
She said "Babe, you already are"
And the members of that team
Went chasing their own dreams

She did not clean the house for hours
She did not rearrange the flowers
No kids to send to school
No living by traditional rules

So as she drove through Paris in a sports car
With the warm wind in her hair
She envied Lucy Jordan
In her daddy's easy chair...

Experiencing

I told Blue-Eyes that it is all about balance. It is knowing what will make you happy at any particular point in time, but also in the greater scheme of things. At times it is going to be all about career, at other times it is going to be all about family. At times it is about learning, at times it is about moving forward and at other times it is about consolidation and setting foundations for the next forward surge. There is never going to be a perfect balance between all the aspects of life, for example career, family, growth, learning, being creative, at any one particular time! It is a constant balancing act where you have to compromise and prioritise. If something is missing, go out and try to get it. Have patience, however, as balance does not mean having it all at once!

"Wishing relates to the end, choice to the means; for instance, we wish to be healthy but do we choose the acts which will make us healthy? We wish to be happy and say we do, but we cannot well say we choose to be so. For in general, choice seems to relate to the things that are in our own power."
Aristotle. *The Complete Works of Aristotle*

In her twenties, Blue-Eyes loved the buzz of the business world. She spent her days outsmarting competitors, creating team spirit and developing winning strategies. Before she knew it, her career had taken over her life. This was not a problem because it provided her with everything that she needed at the time. She travelled extensively. She met interesting people. She got her first BMW. She hoped that one day she would be able to achieve a better balance, but until that day she decided to focus on her career.

She learnt that customers were not always right! They can only react as their personality and understanding of things permits or as I put it, they can only react on their own level of being. It is a skill to educate them, to create a need that they did not know they had, and to use modern day jargon, to sell into their buying window.

"If I had asked customers what they wanted they would have said a faster horse". Henry Ford

In the corporate world, it is easy to think that every promotion, every salary increase and every pat on the back is a direct reflection of one's worth. There are endless meetings where one's worth is re-confirmed and where participants assure one another of their respective importance.

A career does not have to be formed in a corporate environment. Some individuals are fortunate enough that they can turn a unique talent or passion into a career. They are blessed, for if you love what you do, you never have to work.

As careers involve ladders to be climbed and competitive people, there will always be some degree of "politics" involved. When she got hurt or upset, I taught Blue-Eyes what I call the "Sandpit-rule". Always view the situation as though you are watching children play in a sandpit. If you take that helicopter view, you can see all the characters playing their parts and you can have empathy and understanding for the behaviour of others. You will also be able to remove the emotion and deal with the situation from an elevated perspective, rather than being too caught up in it and most importantly, you can prevent getting sand in your eyes!

In my role as guardian angel I have witnessed that one of the greatest contributors to happiness is to be fulfilled in your vocation, even if the material rewards are minimal. One of the greatest contributors to bitterness is to realise that your vocation has come to nothing, even if you are materially successful.

There is much to be said for having a career. You learn new skills, you are constantly challenged, and if you are lucky you meet mentors who can help you understand new philosophies and new ways to live. Blue-Eyes met many managers on her journey, but only a few mentors. Mentors are individuals who not only excel at what they do, they have enormous enthusiasm and the ability to impart their knowledge and experience as well as the ability to coach and bring out the best in their subordinates.

I have taught Blue-Eyes that there is a great difference between Managers and Leaders. Managers do things right, whereas Leaders do the right things. Managers tell people what to do, whereas Leaders inspire the right actions.

One of the greatest examples of a true leader is Nelson Mandela. In 2008 when he was ninety years old, he was interviewed for Time Magazine by Richard Stengel, where Mr Mandela defines his rules of Leadership:

Nelson Mandela's wisdom on Leadership teaches that courage is not the absence of fear, but it is inspiring people to move beyond fear. You have to lead from the front, but ensure to bring others with you on your journey otherwise you will leave them behind. It is even more important to lead from the back and let others believe that they are in front. Mr Mandela would often just listen, clarifying his thoughts before subtly steering the decision in the direction he wanted it to go. He thought it was important to know the enemy: he learnt to speak Afrikaans and he brushed up on his knowledge of rugby (Afrikaners' beloved sport). He neutralised his rivals with charm and was always smiling. Mr Mandela was comfortable with contradiction. He would always have the end goal in mind and seek the most practical way to get there. He knew when to quit, knowing that this was leading too.

With Nelson Mandela as inspiration, I have taught Blue-Eyes to learn and witness the art of negotiation and leadership. Traditional thinking would make you believe that whoever has the most power wins. Effective negotiation, however, shows that no power, or creating the illusion of no power, wins. The biggest obstacle in effective negotiation skills is having a big ego. Enter the negotiation with humility, good listening skills, deflect emotion, and always have a fall-back position. A true artist in effective negotiation skills is fearless without showing it, has the end result in sight, and will make the other party believe they came up with the solution whilst achieving the desired result.

"Once there lived a village of creatures along the bottom of a great crystal river. The current of the river swept silently over them all – young and old, rich and poor, good and evil, the current going its own way, knowing only its own crystal self. Each creature in its own manner clung tightly to the twigs and rocks of the river bottom, for clinging was their way of life, and resisting the current what each had learned from birth. But one creature said at last, 'I am tired of clinging. Though I cannot see it with my eyes, I trust that the current knows where it is going. I shall let go, and let it take me where it will. Clinging, I shall die of boredom.' The other creatures laughed and said, 'Fool! Let go, and that current you worship will throw you tumbled and smashed across the rocks, and you will die quicker than boredom!' But the one heeded them not and taking a breath did let go, and at once was tumbled and smashed by the current across the rocks. Yet in time, as the creature refused to cling again, the current lifted him free from the bottom, and he was bruised and hurt no more. And the creatures downstream, to whom he was a stranger cried, 'See a miracle! A creature like ourselves, yet he flies! See the Messiah, come to save us all!' And the one carried in the current said, 'I am no more Messiah than you. The river

delights to lift us free, if only we dare let go. Our true work is this voyage, this adventure." Richard Bach. *Illusions*

The next step in Blue-Eyes' career was international re-location. She considered it such an honour to be one of the youngest ex-pats in the organisation and jumped at the opportunity. The decision was easy.

"Indecision is like a stepchild: If he does not wash his hands, he is called dirty, if he does, he is wasting water". African Proverb

To relocate meant more travel, more interesting people to meet and the opportunity to gain international experience. She was afraid, leaving behind her comfort zone. A comfort zone is exactly that – comfortable! She now had to leave behind her friends, family and support structure and move to the unknown. She was based in the UK, but travelled all over the world. Some trips were great, others merely tiring. She soon discovered that business travel is not as glamorous as one would think. The insides of a car, hotel room, plane or boardroom look very similar, anywhere in the world.

Blue-Eyes' first year in her new country was the hardest. On her first birthday abroad, she came home from the office and found faxes scattered all over the floor and emails and messages from friends and family at home. At the office they did not know it was her birthday. She had never felt so alone in her whole life. She sat crying on the floor and nearly packed her bags, but I was holding her close. I told her she had to be brave, she had to let go in order to open up for new opportunities of growth and happiness to enter her life.

"Difficulties are precisely what make change and ascent possible. Without them we should all have gone to permanent

sleep long ago." Rodney Collin. *The Theory of Conscious Harmony.*

"Sometimes, by letting go we allow some grace to enter by another channel, which all our mental efforts have hitherto kept out". Rodney Collin. *The Theory of Conscious Harmony.*

Although such an experience as re-locating to a foreign country can be exciting, it is also incredibly daunting! Arriving in a new place where you don't know anyone is scary. You have no support structure, and you have to give a lot of yourself to make new friends and integrate and get a new life. Some take the easy option of falling in with the local expat community from their own countries, but the point is to experience the local culture and the benefit is that you can re-invent yourself as a stronger and better person. The downside is that you soon become a hybrid with a lack of identity – Blue-Eyes was no longer totally South African and she was also not totally British. I whispered to her that she was a "Child of the Universe" and as the world is getting "smaller" and people are migrating more, there are a whole new generation that are children of the universe.

In her late twenties, Blue-Eyes was starting to question the lack of balance in her life as her entire being revolved around work and career. There is nothing wrong with working hard, but something was missing and she thought that there had to be a better balance and realised that she was lonely. At this stage of her journey she simply played the cards she was dealt, hoping that she would find a better balance and trying to be patient with all that was unresolved in her heart.

Experiencing

CONTRAST

Running, sitting, waiting
Tired to the bone
Left brain exhausted
Right brain create a poem

Life is full of irony
Experiences of adversity
Contrast a certainty
Confusion a reality

Success
Achievement
Choice
Bereavement

Prioritise
Compromise
Capitalise
Improvise

Born with a career path
No-one to call home
Surrounded by people
Always alone

Equipped to be mobile
Difficult to move
Owned by shareholders
So much to prove

Freedom, excitement
Dedication, control
Intellectual stimulation
Mostly on a roll

Lifestyle addictive
Lifestyle restrictive
Financial reward
Emotionless, bored

Searching

Chapter 5:
SEARCHING

"Remember that you behave as at a banquet. Is anything brought round to you? Put out your hand and take a moderate share. Doth it pass you by? Do not stop it. Is it not yet come? Do not yearn in desire towards it, but wait until it reaches you. Be so with regard to children, spouse, office, and riches and you will sometime be worthy to feast with the Gods." **Epictetus.** The Discourses, a Classical Guide to Freedom and Happiness.

On their journey through life, humanity searches for many things. They search for answers to their many questions. It would be so easy for us angels to provide the answers, but our children must live the questions and evolve into the answers, that is part of what develops them and makes them grow as individuals. Sometimes, when answers are sought, we do provide answers or solutions. Someone may be struggling with an issue and a friend may contact them out of the blue with a suggestion, this of course is no coincidence. Inspiration, answers and ideas may come from strange sources, and what seems like coincidence springs from divine intervention or the deepest source of destiny.

Humanity searches for happiness and fulfilment. They search for knowledge and enlightenment. They search for achievement, although some are happy with success. As guardian angel I have witnessed that the difference is that success is what other people think of you whilst achievement is what you think of yourself.

They have debates about choice and religion. Religion is immensely personal with individual searches leading to different answers.

In the different religions there are a lot of "man-made" rules. Religions do require rules and discipline. However, it is easy to get confused by these man-made rules, or to use them as excuses not to believe at all. It is much harder to search for and find what you consider to be the truth. If you don't like a particular Church, search until you find one that feeds your soul. Like any other, a relationship with God requires work and an investment of time.

"The thought of God – most neglected in life of all humanity's attributes, easily covered with dust, deluded and abused, rejected, yet the only certain source of what all are seeking, but few or none find." Walt Whitman. *Leaves of Grass.*

"However much we are attracted and fascinated by the myriad phenomena of this earth, an inner longing compels us again and again to turn our eye heavenward because an inexplicable deep feeling convinces us that we are citizens of those worlds that mysteriously shine above us and that we shall someday return thither." J.W. von Goethe. *Johann Wolfgang von Goethe.*

"A thought – the thought that wakes in silent hours – perhaps the deepest, most eternal thought latent in the human soul – this is the thought of God, merged in the thoughts of moral right and the immortality of identity. Great, great is this thought – aye, greater than all else. Walt Whitman. *Leaves of Grass.*

Fate is a Western idea, derived from the three Abrahamic religions, Judaism, Christianity and Islam. It means that a force outside oneself has an influence on one's life. Christianity teaches that man was made in the image of God with a personality and the ability to receive and give love and make choices and have a free will.

The Eastern philosophy of karma means roughly making one's own fate through cause and effect.

"No one escapes destiny." Plato. *Complete Works by Plato.*

"There is no such thing as chance; and what seems to us the merest accident springs from the deepest source of destiny." Friedrich Schiller. *The Aesthetic Letters, Essays, and the Philosophical Letters of Schiller.*

Humanity searches for friendship and kindness. Having moved to a new country, at first Blue-Eyes did not know many people. A friend from work introduced her to the "Cheshire Princesses". They were a group of women who all had very busy lives and believed in the work hard and play hard philosophy. Amongst the group there was a solicitor, conveyor, marketing director and owner of her own company as well as a few others. They were mostly blonde. They were mostly single. They were funny, experienced and interesting. They didn't know it, but they saved her in so many ways. They brought fun back into her life. They gave her a sense of belonging, but mostly they gave her friendship.

CHESHIRE PRINCESSES

E-Mails and phone calls
Building up to Friday night
Excitement, anticipation
The future looks bright

Six blondes and a brunet
Make up the Cheshire set
Modern princesses gathering
Reality easy to forget

Independent and gorgeous
Sweet and glamorous
Crowned with intelligence and charm
Protecting each other from harm

Adhere to only a few rules
To be generous
To be gorgeous
To live life to the fullest

No conventional women
No regrets
Many secrets

A girlie world of make believe
Free from pain or any grief
Secretly hoping this will be the night
For prince charming to turn into Mr. Right

Princesses who have been around
Know frogs must be kissed before princes are found
Learned to live with no despair
Knowing the girls will always be there!

Following friendship, most people's primary search on their journey through life is for love. To find that one person that can be a witness to their journey, and who will make the journey more enjoyable.

The Cheshire Princesses had a lot of things in common but the most obvious was their individual search for a Prince. Mostly on their search, they kept meeting frogs.

PRESENCE

Electricity
Presence
A sense of knowing
Making me defenceless

As the walls come tumbling down
I build them up again
I don't make any sense of this
Adding to my frustration

What will happen if we kiss?
Will we spin out of control?
Will he run away?
Or will he be brave enough to stay?

Humanity is often confused by the meaning of love. They are searching for that person that is going to make them happy, healthy and complete. In order to be capable of loving, one must be able to love oneself. In order to be able to receive love, one must be able to give love and happiness. One must be happy within oneself.

"Love and be bold; for he that dies hath these for wings to rise from earth to heaven." Michelangelo Buonarroti. *Complete Poems and Selected Letters of Michelangelo.*

LOVE: the little word that means so much but is so frequently abused and misused.

1 Corinthians 13:4-13. ***"Love is patient, love is kind. It does not envy, it does not boast, it is not proud. It is not rude, it is not self-seeking, it is not easily angered, it keeps no record of wrongs. Love does not delight in evil but rejoices with the truth. It always protects, always trusts, always hopes, always perseveres….and now these three remain: faith, hope and love. But the greatest of these is love."***

Blue-Eyes wanted to meet her soul mate just like anybody else. She wanted to meet her prince, but for some reason he kept escaping her. She thought that perhaps her standards were too high. Quite a few frogs got moulded into the ideal prince. If it was up to her alone, she would have settled for a frog, and I had to try and teach her to be patient, to have faith and to have hope.

ALL I REALLY WANT

To win the fight
To always be right
Someone who loves me
The right to be crazy

A night at the Ritz
A friend with benefits
Travelling on week ends
Having mutual friends

Quality time
Aura's that rhyme
Intellectual intercourse
Passion that soars

Even though we share affection
I demand more attention
So it's time to decide
Multiply or divide

If you want me to go
Then say it
If you want me to stay
Then show it

I live with no regrets
I deserve some damn respect
As we're reaching the end of the line
Just be honest this one time

Why are you so afraid?
Like a crab that runs sideways
Clinging to the rock
Not wanting to take stock

Searching

'Cause if you do you might just find
You think your ensuring peace of mind
But as time is slipping by
Sentenced to boredom like watching paint dry

I have bared my naked soul
Hope you enjoyed the show
All I really want is to know
Should I stay or should I go?

Frog's reply…

Should you stay or should you go?
Am I the one supposed to know?

I am that crab who needs to cling
I shrink with fear when changes ring

Equipped for moving side to side
Crabs lack the tools to help decide

Forward or back, how does that go?
Let's not rush now, take it slow…

Living in a never land
Trying hard to understand
The meaning of it all

Sometimes it's so hard to tell
Stuck inside this bloody shell

"One must not try to cling to opportunities which have come, however pleasant and comforting. For that is the way to kill them. Let good things go without regret. Then better ones may come." *Rodney Collin – The Theory of Conscious Harmony.*

Blue-Eyes got tired of the dating game. She stopped searching for "IT."

IT

Everybody's looking for IT
To love, to share
The IT Embargo
This love-hate phenomenon that we can't let go

Go out on we hate them nights
Yet talk about them all the time
Tired of the dating game
The questions and answers are all the same

Maybe expectations are too high
Maybe IT's there if we really try
But why settle for second best?
Just to be with someone like all the rest

I want someone to make me whole
To be my friend and make my toes curl
To feed the starvation
To share the affection
To be the first to hear my news
To get the last kiss before I close my eyes

To share the laughter
To wipe away the tears
To give me hugs
Remove all the fears

Why is IT so difficult to find?
Lifestyle, career, stubbornness, closed mind?
I have stopped looking, setting myself free
Hoping, one day, IT will find me

Believing

Chapter 6:
BELIEVING

"Sometimes, by letting go we allow some grace to enter by another channel, which all our mental efforts have hitherto kept out." Rodney Collin – The theory of Conscious Harmony

One of our biggest challenges is to teach humanity how to have faith, hope, and patience! There is a lot that must happen in the background before everything just "falls into place". Often someone will say, "It was just fate" without realising all the effort that took place for fate to happen.

Someone may look at their life and recognise all the uncanny coincidences. They may acknowledge some miraculous moments. Everyone has at least one magical tale to tell. It is up to us guardian angels to ensure that humanity recognise "meant to be" and guide them in times of doubt and confusion.

It is often like a child on a bicycle with dad's hand on the back. Once he gets going on a certain path, he builds up speed and confidence and sets forth! Often the road he's on is not the right one, or he may not know of some obstacles up ahead so dad catches up with him and picks him up, bike and all. This is accompanied by kicking and screaming because he liked the road he was on, he was doing so well. When the wheels touch the ground again and he is pointed in the right direction, off he goes building up speed and reeling with delight, until the next change of direction....

I have pointed out to Blue-Eyes, and others, that they constantly behave like the child in the air, kicking and screaming once they are forced to change direction. "Some people seem to ride forever without stopping," they argue. Why do they not have the patience

Believing

to stop and be pointed in the right direction? Why is it so difficult to be extremely grateful that they have a Father who cares enough to interfere when they are not on the right path? Why is it so difficult for humanity to have faith or to "Faith it out"?

I BELIEVE

I believe in the future
I believe in happiness
I believe in love
I believe...

Is the fairy-tale ending?
Does the bus stop here
Or is this the beginning
New opportunities near

In these uncertain times
Trying to be brave
Has the star shone too brightly?
Can it be saved?

Showing off the photographs
Of years gone past
Looking at the autographs
Of all the lives touched

Lived in many places
Friendly smiles, warm embraces
Fond memories
Many stories

> Reached a stage
> Where choices need to be made
> If choices are half chance
> Who chooses the music for the next dance?
>
> So many facets to life
> Avenues to explore
> Why is it so difficult?
> To open comfort zone's door
>
> If the constant is change
> What else remains?
> But faithing it out
> Isn't that what life's all about?
>
> I still believe...

Blue-Eyes realised that there were many times when she would have made the wrong decisions, or would have settled for second best as a result of being too impatient and not having faith. I had to carry her kicking and screaming (without her realising of course) onto a different path many times. This was certainly the case with regard to jobs she wanted and did not get, or more importantly, partners she wanted and did not get. I was working very hard behind the scenes to find her prince and to align everything in the universe for them to meet and to fall in love.

She had just about lost faith and given up all hope that she would find the person with whom she wanted to spend the rest of her life. I had to drag her out with the girls one Saturday evening. As always they were causing quite a commotion in the corner of the restaurant, when her prince walked in with his friend. It was just before eleven pm when Blue-Eyes looked up and straight into his eyes. Her heart physically skipped a beat. They were staring at each other for what felt like eternity as everything in the universe aligned to make that moment possible. They both started to smile and it was as though nothing in the past mattered and as though the future looked so much brighter. Although they were strangers, they had a familiarity which was born from the deepest sources of destiny. Blue-Eyes walked over and said to him, "What are you laughing at? You are the one in the pink shirt." The next day he sent her a scarf from the Thomas Pink shop in pink packaging with a card that read: "In time, you will learn to think pink."

They got engaged three months later. It was love at first sight, it was perfect, and it was easy. It was meant to be. It was a miracle. They did not need to know about all the hard work and all the effort that we as angels had to put in to make that moment possible and to create that miracle.

Many people say: "You just know." Somehow, you just know when you are fortunate enough to meet THE one that is meant for you as part of your destiny.

Blue-Eyes always used mind maps as a thinking technique. She made these spider web-type drawings on a piece of paper, which is a brilliant tool for brainstorming or remembering things. The creative side of the brain is forced to work with the logical side; thus the brain is used more effectively. She once made a mind map of her ideal man. She read somewhere that knowing what you wanted was halfway to getting it. This was something to do with knowing exactly what your goals are, as you then can be more focused in achieving them. Her mind map of her ideal man was done years before she met her prince and when she read it again, having met him, it was a perfect description of him.

MINDMAP

You live, you learn
You search, you yearn
You explore, you burn
You do mindmaps, you earn?

In learning, you add to the list
Yet the basics remain
Like shooting for a target
Perfecting one's aim

When you realise it is within reach
Fall into place the final piece
Life's greatest gift
The perfect fit

Blue-Eyes could still not believe that IT could happen to her.

Believing

CAN IT BE TRUE

Can it be true?
That the dream could come true
That the fairy-tale exists
Which we can't resist

Can it be true?
That since I've met you
The picture unfolds
The story behold

Can it be true?
That knowing you
The tree bears fruit
The clouds removed?

Can it be true?
That love is real
Happiness forever
As long as we're together

Loving

Chapter 7:
LOVING

"When love beckons to you, follow him, though his ways are hard and steep. And when his wings enfold you yield to him, though the sword hidden among his pinions may wound you. And when he speaks to you believe in him. Though his voice may shatter your dreams as the north wind lays waste the garden. For even as love crowns you so shall he crucify you. Even as he is for your growth so is he for your pruning…But if in your fear you would seek only love's peace and love's pleasure, then it is better for you that you cover your nakedness and pass out of love's threshing-floor. Into the seasonless world where you shall laugh, but not all of your laughter, and weep, but not all of your tears. Love gives naught but itself and takes naught but from itself. Love possesses not nor would it be possessed; for love is sufficient unto love." Kahlil Gibran – *The Prophet*

The invitation to the wedding of Blue-Eyes and her prince read as follows:

> By accident they met
> By accident in love
> Or was it the hands of fate?
> Guardian Angels from up above
>
> Rolling dice from important hands
> For hearts from different lands
> And fate was sealed
> It is now revealed
>
> With faith true love will conquer
> And more than chance will decide
> When rainbow nation's daughter
> And England's son unite
>
> So join us in this dance
> To celebrate this platinum romance
> True love will guide the way
> Come join our wedding day
>
> © Robert & Annette Forster

They got married on a snowy day in December in the British Lake District. They were married in a beautiful little chapel next to a lake and although it was one of the coldest days of the year, it was the warmest day of their lives.

Loving

A song by Don Henley, written by Larry John McNally seemed very appropriate.

"For My Wedding" by Larry John McNally:

To want what I have
To take what I'm given with grace
For this I pray
On my wedding day

For my wedding, I don't want violins
Or sentimental songs about
Thick and thin
I want a moment of silence
And a moment of prayer
For the love we'll need to make it
In the world out there...

Family and friends travelled across the globe to share in their happiness. Their wedding day was filled with music and poetry and special moments. There were candles and lots of lilies and the angels rejoiced.

HAPPY EVER AFTER [2]

The colour of her eyes was like the ocean
But the colour of her heart was just as blue
She thought that love had finally found her
    But now grey skies surround her
She don't know what she's gonna do

But all those boys they were mistaken
And the friends she never knew at school
    They were looking at the cover
    They weren't looking at the other
But the other part makes a woman true

    And oh she gets so lonely
    And oh she gets so cold

But she still believes in fairy tales and a dress of white
    A handsome prince on a starry night
    And though the reasons don't seem right
    And when she can't say
She knows happy ever after is on its way

Now she's grown and things are different
And men they queue to play their part
But though she's beautiful and free now
She don't have freedom of the heart

    And oh she gets so lonely
    And oh she gets so cold

---

2. Permission granted by Robert Forster to publish lyrics of this song in full.

Loving

> But she still believes in fairy tales and a dress of white
> A handsome prince on a starry night
> And though the reasons don't seem right
> And when she can't say
> She knows happy ever after is on its way
>
> Then one day it seemed from nowhere
> In he rode to save the day
> Didn't seem like nothing special
> But that girl knew straight away
> She'd be loving him someday
>
> The colour of her eyes is like the ocean
> But now her heart burns like the sun
> And though you know she's had some hard times
> She don't regret a single one
> Cause look what that girls just gone and done
> She used to be so lonely
> She used to be so cold
>
> But she still believed in fairy tales and a dress of white
> A handsome prince on a starry night
>
> He came one day and made it right
> And now she can say
> Happy Ever After starts today
> Happy Ever After is here to stay
>
> © Robert Forster

Blue-Eyes realised that she had finally found 'IT' or rather; it had found her.

IT HAPPENS

She saw in his eyes
What she had never seen
Kindness, sincerity, happiness
The awakening of a dream

He's got eyes like the ocean
A soul that's just as deep
Fun, laughter, seriousness
Guarding her when she sleeps

She thought she was a worldly girl
Independent and free
Then she dived into the ocean
And she drowned in the sea

She awakened in a different world
To the one she's known before
The principles remain
The content means so much more

What used to be important
Vaporised into the sun
The heat of love is all consuming
The future has just begun

She never realised what she was missing
Never knew she was incomplete
Never noticed the coldness around her
Until she experienced the heat

He's got eyes like the ocean
A soul that's just as deep
And only in drowning
Was she made complete

It is a miracle to find one's other half. It is a miracle to love somebody unconditionally and to be loved in the same way. It is a miracle to be with someone with whom one is so compatible. It is ultimately God's greatest gift to be given a partner that can be a witness to your life, the good and the bad, the happy and the sad.

Matthew 19:5-6 "For this reason a man will leave his father and mother and be united to his wife, and the two will become one flesh. So they are no longer two, but one. Therefore what God has joined together let man not separate."

BEFORE YOU CAME 3

Before you came
The skies were blue
And the sun would shine
The birds would sing
And the church bells chime
Smiles would crack
And laughter sound
The world would turn
The seasons creep round

BUT WHEN YOU CAME

Skies would shine like a sapphire ring
With radiance and wonder the day would bring
Colours would blind with brilliance and sharpness
A kiss of light in a forest of darkness

---

3. Permission granted by Robert Forster to publish poem.

JOURNEY

The sun would rise like a mighty King
With rays of messengers with life to bring
The earth would bow at its fiery court
With flowers of life the offerings sought

Birds no longer soloists would be
But like orchestrated Angles praising in harmony
With sounds as gentle as a butterfly's wing
But as powerful as thunder their opera's sing

And bells from churches would chime their story
Like their steepled homes pronounce loves glory
And scales of wonder would mark their range
As archangels and saints ovation each change

Smiles no longer would hint and creep
But rise like daybreak, and race and leap
As the heart would snuggle and tickle and twist
No gloom of sadness could just resist

Laughter would roar like lions caged
The eternal truth could not be aged
And even as night led its blackest hour
Loves smiles of light would surely devour

The world no longer would ache and turn
But spin, fly and fizz as chains would burn
And while natures rules and laws constrain
The science of love no shackles restrain

The elements of universe would merge and create
No longer separate, divides to contemplate
A merger, an alliance of earth's greatest foes
Earth, wind and fire lay down their bows

Loving

> For love will demand the highest prize
> As joy not pain tear their eyes
>
> Before you came....
> The world was waiting
> An uncertain child anticipating
> Like a helping hand you calmed the tide
> A destiny you would provide
>
> Before you came
> I could,
> Now I can.
> After you came
> My world began.
>
> © Robert Forster

It is naive to think that love is only to provide peace and pleasure. Love possesses the power to hurt, to damage and to destroy if not treated with dignity and respect. A partnership build on love holds up a mirror to one's faults, and as love is for your growth it is also for your pruning. Only true love will withstand the scrutiny, the pain, the highs and the lows, the temptations and the learning that comes from being in a long term relationship. For true love lets you laugh with all of your laughter and weep with all of your tears. True love loves with all of your soul and leaves you vulnerable and exposed. Just as you must know hunger before you can appreciate a feast, just as you must feel parched before water can quench your thirst, so you must know agony in order to appreciate ecstasy. If you can accept love with all it has to offer, you will bask in its glory.

LOVE

Love is a feeling
Of being whole
Love is contentment
Losing control

Love is when the past
Turns into a vague memory
When today and tomorrow
Become the only reality

Love is when you are
Where you want to be
When completeness and happiness
Are there for all to see

Love is a challenge
It's the ultimate gift
Love is surrender
It's not a defeat

Love is unselfish
Love is kind
Love is all consuming
Love is blind

Love is trust
Love is sincere
Even when miles apart
You are always near

Loving

Love is the answer
To everyone's prayers
Never to be taken for granted
Knowing someone cares

Love is faith
A warm embrace
Being lost and found
Accept it with grace

Love knows no sacrifice
Love has no compromise
Love is wanting to give more than one can
Love is being your biggest fan

Creating

Photograph by Milo Keely*
*Permission granted by Milo Keely to publish image

Chapter 8:
CREATING

"If you don't follow through on your creative ideas, someone else will pick them up and use them. When you get an idea of this sort, you should jump in with both feet, not just stick your toe in the water... Be daring, be fearless and don't be afraid that somebody is going to criticise you or laugh at you. If your ego is not involved no one can hurt you." GURU R.H.H.
Talk Does not Cook the Rice

Angels like to create harmony and understanding. At times, we can be a bit more creative. Blue-Eyes wanted her engagement ring and their wedding rings made in South Africa. Rings are round, endless and throughout history are used when a couple gets engaged/promised to one another, and during the wedding ceremony as a symbol of their love and devotion. The rings are symbols that a couple make a lifelong covenant, putting on the rings when saying their vows. Both partners should wear and respect those symbols.

This symbolism is included in most wedding ceremonies:

- *Church of England (1662 Book of Common Prayer) -* **"With this ring I thee wed, with my body I thee worship, and with all my worldly goods I thee endow: In the Name of the Father, and of the Son, and of the Holy Ghost. Amen"**
- *Church of England – Traditional words for the exchange of rings:* **"With my body I honour you, all that I am I give to you, and all that I have I share with you, within the love of God, Father, Son and Holy Spirit"**
- *Jewish -* **"With this ring, you are consecrated to me according to the law of Moses and Israel."**
- *Roman Catholic -* **"… take this ring as a sign of my**

love and fidelity. In the name of the Father, and of the Son, and of the Holy Spirit."

Back to the rings and being creative, Blue-Eyes and her prince visited jewellers in South Africa. They were shown a selection of diamonds, all different and unique with different price tags attached. One particular stone caught her eye and she could not help looking at it, regardless of the price. Her prince had a certain amount of savings stashed away for such a day. These savings did not cover the stone she kept looking at. I had a quick word with Jhudiel (her prince's guardian angel) and when her prince asked the store owner to write down a formal quotation for the diamond and setting that she liked, he wrote down the exact amount that her prince had saved in his bank account back in the UK for this purpose. Before our "creativity" could be noticed, the ring was ordered and paid for and we smiled when Blue-Eyes and her prince discussed if this was a very strange coincidence or if it was divine intervention.

Many years later, on a cold autumn evening with leaves and puddles covering most surfaces outside, Blue-Eyes lost her wedding ring during a night out. She was obviously very distraught. She decided that she would go searching through the mud and in the dark, even if it took all night. She took her coat, her torch and her steely determination and set off in the dark. I knew what this meant to her and as she was praying to God, I showed her exactly where the ring was. She found it in the middle of a road, in a dark car park surrounded by piles of leaves. It was as dark as a November night in England could be after midnight but she saw the light as she hold the ring close to her heart. The ring was round, endless, marked but intact. It was slightly battered as cars must have driven over it but she thought that now, more than ever it was a true symbol of a marriage.

More often, our creativity is focused on nurturing the creativity in humanity.

"The creative individual not only respects the irrational in himself, but courts the most promising source of novelty in his own thought… The creative person is both primitive and more cultured, more destructive and more constructive, crazier and saner, than the average person." Frank Barron. *Creative Person and Creative Process.*

Humanity creates ideas, businesses, music, art, architecture. To create is to leave a legacy for the future and it takes many forms. The most precious of all creation is to create children, the greatest responsibility and achievement of any human being. Some do not realise the importance of parenthood, the precious gift of a child and the responsibility of caring for and guiding them. Just like we look after and protect and inspire our children, so much more is the responsibility of a parent having a child.

Matthew 18:10 "Be careful. Don't think these little children are worth nothing. I tell you that they have angels in heaven who are always with my Father in heaven."

Individuals only become truly vulnerable when they have children. You have to look your children in the eyes and explain your actions. You can achieve greatness as an individual which will be spoken about but the unspoken greatness belongs to individuals who realise that their most important role is to ensure the happiness and well-being of their children.

"You are the bows from which your children as living arrows are sent forth. The archer sees the mark upon the path of the infinite, and He bends you with His might that His arrows may go swift and far. Let your bending in the archer's hand

be for gladness; For even as he loves the arrow that flies, so He loves also the bow that is stable". Khalil Gibran – *The Prophet.*

The most important role models for parents are their own parents. That does not mean that people from dysfunctional backgrounds cannot be good parents, every person has a free will. If you are blessed with having a child, every decision and action that you take on a daily basis impacts upon the happiness and well-being of an innocent being. That is such a privilege and such a responsibility. A parent's love should be unconditional and a child should respect and appreciate that love.

As guardian angel I have witnessed that the greatest gifts parents can give their children are roots and wings. Always being there for their children and always being supportive.

MA

Altyd beskeie, vriendelik en geduldig
Deugsaam en vol liefde
Ons het so baie aan Ma verskuldig

Ma se woorde en dade het ons nog altyd inspireer
Al Ma se kinders
Monumente van die eer

Ma se wense vir ons is legio
Ons het genoeg wysheid en ondersteuning
Om 'n blink toekoms te bou

Ma wens vir ons genoeg sukses om ons te laat wen
Genoeg teleurstelling, om ons teer te hou
Genoeg stilte om God te leer ken

Dankie vir die monumente van herinnering
Lang kuiers in die kombuis
Beskuit en koffie in die bed gebring

Pannekoekop Vrydae aande toe ons jonger was
Nagsoene en trooswoorde
Wanneer ons moeg of seer was

Nou het ons kookkos op Sondae
Lang geselse oor selfone
En die wete – Ma is altyd daar!

Voorbeeld van 'n Moeder en die "Deugsame vrou"
Hoe 'n wonderlike voorreg om te se "Dankie"
En op die sukses voort te bou

Creating

The English translation of the poem:

MOTHER

Always humble, friendly and patient
Virtuous and full of love
We owe you so much

Your words and deeds always inspired us
All your children
Are monuments of this honour

Your wishes for us are legendary
We have the wisdom and support
To build a bright future

You want us to have enough success to make us win
Enough disappointment to keep us humble
Enough silence to get to know God

Thank you for the memories
Long chats in the kitchen
Rusks and coffee brought to us in bed

Pancakes on Fridays when we were younger
Kisses and kind words
When we were tired or unwell

Now we have Sunday lunches
Long chats on cell phones
And the knowledge, mum is always there!

Example of a mother and a virtuous woman
What a privilege to say thank you
And to continue building on your success

When a child is born, all the angels rejoice!

"What you've given me" *by David Budget*[4]

And so a Mother, holds her child
For the first time, in her arms
Sticky lids, open wide
As new eyes and old are found

Tears are streaming down her face
As emotion fills the place
That's what you are here for
That's what you are here for
That's what you are here for, my love
And what you've given me, completes me

Now get some sleep, you must be weak
It's been a long night, I hope you're alright
I'll stay with you and hold your hand
Watch over you two, in wonderland

Now tears are streaming down my face
As emotion fills my space
That's what I am here for
That's what I am here for
That's what I am here for, my love
And what you've given me, completes me

Now on this day, I'm overcome
On how we've made our little one
Those rosy cheeks, and smiling eyes will
Forever make me realise

---

4. Permission granted by David Budget to publish lyrics of this song in full.

Creating

>Just what has taken place
>Our happiness, your grace
>That's what we are here for
>That's what we are here for
>That's what we are here for, my love
>And what you've given me,
>Completes me.
>
>©David Budget

"*The baby rises to its feet, takes a step, is overcome with triumph and joy – and falls flat on its face. It is a pattern for all that is to come! But learn from the bewildered baby. Lurch to your feet again. You'll make the sofa in the end.*" Pam Brown. *The Swish of the Curtain.*

FATHER

You stand beside us
You take each by the hand
You're strength is to guide us

Everything you've done was the best for us
We didn't always understand
Yet you always loved us

Endless encouragement
Unconditional love
The greatest gifts you gave us

You give us strength
You show us the way
We'd want you as our father, if we ever had a say

You taught us to question
To be independent and free
You inspired our travels, our ambitions and dreams

You believe in us and always show you care
If you scan the acknowledgements
Your name will always be there

In looking at your children
We know you are proud
We are grateful to be able to say thank you out loud

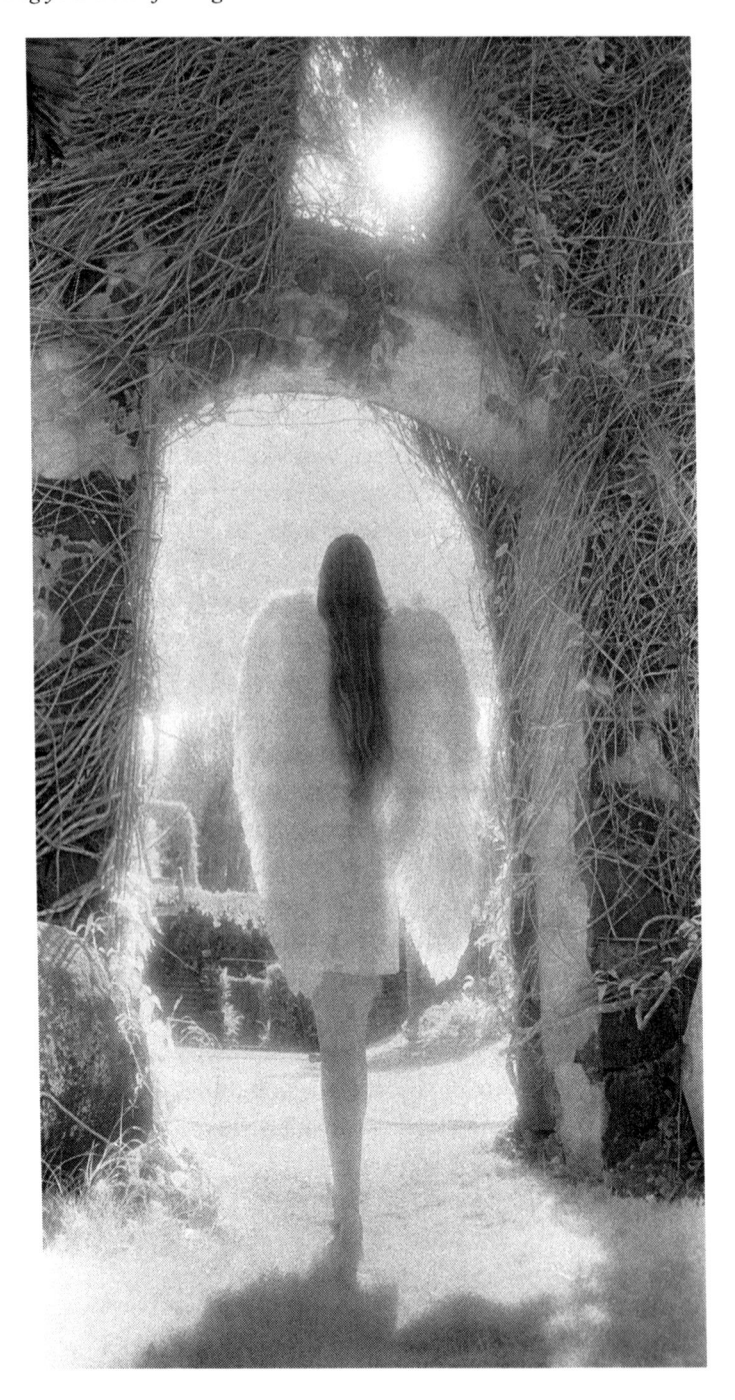

Improving your level of Being

Chapter 9:
IMPROVING YOUR LEVEL OF BEING

"It is not for show that our soul must enact its part; it is at home, within us, where no eyes penetrate but our own." **Michel Montaigne.** *Complete Essays of Montaigne by M.E. De Montaigne.*

I have witnessed fascinating times and through all the technological advancements, all the changes, all the uncertainty, and the increased pace in lifestyle, I can recommend a return to the basics of burning candles, listening to music, discussing values and beliefs and making time stand still. It is important to feed the soul.

Hebrews 13:2 "Remember to welcome strangers, because some who have done this have welcomed angels without knowing it."

Recognise the miracles in everyday life. Continue asking questions and if you don't have the answers, try to live the questions. Your expectations will keep changing. At least you are stretching the boundaries to see how far they will go. To succeed, one must learn to fail. Life will knock you down, that is not important. What is important is how you get up.

TO BE HUMBLE

It's good to know
Our Father still shows
He cares by making us stumble
Just enough to keep us humble

Never take anything for granted
Treasure what is important
Our wiseness will show
Contentment will follow

"You will have wonderful surges forward. Then there must be a time of consolidating before the next forward surge. Accept this as part of the process and never become downhearted."
Eileen Caddy *Footprints on the Path*

There will be times when you are pushed to learn and to grow. All great philosophies say that suffering is part of the human condition and gives strength. God does not want anyone to suffer unnecessarily, so by embracing it and learning from it, one can rise above it.

Sometimes in life it may feel as though you are swimming against the tide. This may be because your guardian angel is steering you in a better direction. When this happens, you have a choice: you can stay on a slow train that will eventually get to the right place, or you can disembark, get a train back to the main station and catch the express. When you are on the express, everything falls into place. You are doing the right things, with the right people for the right reasons. You are heading in the right direction.

"Come to the edge', he said. They said: 'We are afraid'. 'Come to the edge', he said. They came. He pushed them...and they flew." Guillaume Apollinaire, *Selected Writings of Guillaume Apollinaire.*

MOMENT

When the moment is broken
After all has been spoken
Where do we go from here?

What if we've made all the sums
But tomorrow never comes
Where do we go from here?

What if today never goes away
And the broken moment stays
Where do we go from here?

For the past is a memory
And the future is a fantasy
But the moment is here...

On my journey of immortality, I have witnessed life and acquired some insights:

- People from different nationalities may fuss over different issues, yet everybody has similar desires, ambitions and dreams.
- Follow your gut feeling – it's a very powerful tool.
- Sometimes we have to take a step back to go ten steps forward.
- Never take anything for granted.
- Never take love for granted.
- The little things count.

Improving your level of Being

- Let go and then you open up for new opportunities.
- Challenge the comfort zone.
- Challenge the boundaries.
- Have goals: If you know what you want, you are half way to achieving it.
- Take risks.
- Have patience.
- Always give your considered response.
- Read.
- Learn.
- Listen.
- Make time to be still: think!
- Faith it out!
- New doors will open when you didn't even know they existed.
- Live for the moment; plan for the future. Remember it is all about the Moment.
- Remember to smile.
- Dream! Dreams are the promises of what you can become.
- Do not rely on someone else for your happiness. Try to make someone else happy.
- Love somebody.
- Love life.
- Listen to the lyrics.
- Be creative.
- Be positive.
- Be happy.

"Never feel guilty about learning. Never feel guilty about wisdom. That is called enlightenment. You must understand that you have done what you needed to do; it was all necessary. And you made all the right choices – all of them!" RAMTHA

Try not to involve the ego. Try to be humble. You must keep saying Thank You. You must learn to maintain the balance and to make the right choices on your way. You should wish for a moment of silence and save moments for prayer. You should stop focusing on trying to get what you want and try to know who you are. You must lift your level of consciousness and reach for the stars!

A guardian angel's guide to improving your level of being is:

- *Faith*

    "Since faith implies a trusting reliance upon future events or outcomes, it is often taken by its detractors as inevitably synonymous with a belief 'not resting on logical proof or material evidence.'" Wikipedia

- *Courage*

    "Courage does not mean being without fear but it is moving forward (embracing change) in spite thereof" Anon

    "Everyone has talent. What is rare is the courage to follow the talent to the dark place where it leads." Erica Jong

    "A great deal of talent is lost to the world for want of a little courage". Sydney Smith

- *Prayer*

    "But when you pray, go into your room, close the door and pray to your Father, who is unseen. Then your Father, who sees what is done in secret, will reward you." Matthew 6:6

"Ask and it will be given to you, seek and you will find, knock and the door will be opened to you. For everyone who asks receives, he who seeks finds and to him who knocks, the door will be opened." Matthew 7:7

"This is the confidence we have in approaching God, that if we ask anything according to his will, he hears us. And if we know that he hears us – whatever we ask – we know that we have what we asked of him." 1 John 5:14

"I think prayer, or some appeal from the whole heart to a force outside our circle of life which alone can alter things there, is the only possibility in certain insoluble circumstances. But surely we must cry to be shown the way out, to be shown the unseen ladder out of the impass, and be very ready to accept whatever is shown. Then if some new idea, some new light comes into one's heart – as it will – one must be prepared to obey courageously. If one does so, one will be led out of the maze." **Rodney Collin.** The Theory of Conscious Harmony – From the Letters of Rodney Collin

- **Hope**

"But hope that is seen is no hope at all. Who hopes for what he already has? But if we hope for what we do not yet have, we wait for it patiently." Romans 8:24

- **Patience**

"I want to beseech you…to be patient toward all that is unsolved in your heart and to try to love the questions themselves like locked rooms and like books that are written *in a very foreign tongue. Do not now seek the answers, which cannot be given you because you would not be able to live them. And the point is, to live everything. Live the questions now. Perhaps you will then gradually, without noticing it, evolve some distant day into the answer."* **Rainer Maria Rilke.** *Letters to a Young Poet*

"To know how to wait is the great secret of success." **Joseph de Maistre**

- **Action**

"To change one's life: Start immediately, do it flamboyantly – no exceptions." **William James**

"If you move towards your goals…opportunity will find you as a result of your actions." **Stuart Wilde**

"Procrastination is the thief of time." **Edward Young**

"Rome wasn't built in a day, but without that first day it wouldn't have been built at all" **R Forster**

"Whatever you can do, or dream you can, begin it. Boldness has genius, power and magic in it. BEGIN IT NOW." **Goethe**

JUST ME

That I would be interesting
Even if my interests were boring

That I would be loved
Just for being me

If I could have one prayer
That's what my prayer would be

Trying to find my place
Accepting with grace

That I am loved
Just for being me

And that you see
Is enough for me

Anticipating

Chapter 10:
ANTICIPATING

Anticipating

"Much suffering in human life results from a fruitless attempt to retain a note that has already ceased to sound, or to anticipate a note that has not yet sounded." *Rodney Collin – The Theory of Conscious Harmony.*

Heaven is the place that I call home. In heaven, the light is golden and very bright without hurting the eyes. Humanity does not realise it, but you get a glimpse of heaven every time you see a sunrise or sunset. When you stare into the distance and see the golden light, you are witnessing heaven, even if just for a split second. It is only possible to reach heaven in a spiritual state and there are no physical objects or desires. There is no sadness, pain or anger. Humanity likes to fantasize about heaven as a place where all their worldly desires will be fulfilled. However, heaven is exalted high above the earthly desires of humankind. It is hard for humanity to anticipate the magnificence of heaven as the ultimate destination.

There are no guides on how to reach this destination, but there are many pointers on how to enjoy the journey. Keep finding the sunsets and you will be on your way.

As for Blue-Eyes, she now calls herself a Boere-Brit. She is enjoying her family and trying to keep up with technology and career, and somehow find a balance between it all, like so many women have done before her. She hopes the rainbow nation will forget about the past and focus all resources and energy on resolving the many challenges it faces in the future. She admires South Africans for their optimism and courage. She admires her adopted nation for its historical pride and sophistication in the arts, and for finding humour in everything. She admires the British for getting on with it, even when the weather is really bad. She has to remind herself that without the rain, there won't be any rainbows.

Anticipating

Genesis 9:12-13 ***And God said:*** *"This is the sign of the covenant I am making between me and you and every living creature with you, a covenant for all generations to come. I have set my rainbow in the clouds, and it will be the sign of the covenant between me and the earth."*

A WOMAN I THOUGHT I KNEW [5]

Mental activity
Success
A drive of ambition
Compassion
Caring

A woman in a competitive world
Yet not competing
You have a sense of knowing
Totally accepting yourself

The key to being
What God created to be

Your belief
Encourages your direction in life
And when in doubt
You have an unfaltering fashion
In faithing it out

Your manner, motion, mindfulness, music, motivation, mentality
Moves me

© Nicole Bekker

---

5. Permission granted by Nicole Bekker to publish poem.

Luke 22:43 *"An angel from heaven appeared to him and strengthened him"*

Revelation 5:11-12 *"Then I looked and I heard the voices of many angels around the throne... there were thousands and thousands of angels."*

Angels will never minister selfishly or direct attention upon ourselves. We continue to serve anonymously in a manner that assures that all glory goes to God. If humankind looks back at the coincidences in their lives and begins to see something else, perhaps a certain protection or comfort coming at just the right time, they should thank God for the protection and inspiration from the most powerful beings in the universe. We execute God's will in every situation on earth, sometimes as quiet bystanders and sometimes through action, when God demands divine intervention.

Anticipating

DESTINY

There is a time to be happy
There is a time to be sad
A time to be grateful
For new friendships to be had

A time to embrace
And a time to refrain
A time to lose
And a time to gain

Who knows what the future will hold?
Who knows what is destiny?
Who knows how big is the gap
The window of opportunity

And whether or not it is dear to us
The future unfolds, as it should
And all we can do is strive to be happy
Smile as often as we could

Humankind can be sure that angels of God are always near to help, guard, strengthen, protect, guide and inspire. We bring messages of warning and guidance. We provide comfort. Yet humankind becomes so easily discouraged and fearful. Remember to have faith, courage, hope and patience. Remember to pray. Above all, enjoy the journey! Don't just aim for the destination!

JOURNEY

Born with a burning desire
To be fabulous
A need to be better and special and gorgeous

What is inside me that drives me
Creating unnecessary baggage
Heaven forbid being Average

Sometimes pretentious
At times loud and spontaneous
Trying to balance with being generous

Goalposts constantly moving
Always demanding more
Who is keeping score?

Trying to define the boundaries
Never mention conventional
Never stick to traditional

Then dawn a realisation
Life is a journey
Not a destination

It's a skill to be still
When we are constantly moving
Life is a challenge but also rewarding

POEMS BY THE AUTHOR:

(In order of appearance in Journey)
All rights reserved ©2010

1. BEING
2. GOODBYE
3. FIRST LOVE
4. MONACO
5. THANK YOU
6. THE BALLAD OF CAREER LUCY JORDAN
7. CONTRAST
8. CHESHIRE PRINCESSES
9. PRESENCE
10. ALL I REALLY WANT
11. IT
12. I BELIEVE
13. MINDMAP
14. CAN IT BE TRUE?
15. IT HAPPENS
16. LOVE
17. MA
18. FATHER
19. TO BE HUMBLE
20. JUST ME
21. MOMENT
22. DESTINY
23. JOURNEY

OTHER POEMS:

All rights reserved ©2010

1. **A LITTLE PIECE OF PEACE** – Nicole Bekker
2. **INVITATION TO WEDDING** – Robert Forster
3. **BEFORE YOU CAME** – Robert Forster
4. **A WOMAN I THOUGHT I KNEW** – Nicole Bekker

LYRICS AND MUSIC

HAPPY EVER AFTER, Rob Forster
Music & Lyrics by Rob Forster ©2010 ,
Can recommend the album Frozen – available from
www.thehut.com search for Rob Forster

LOVE
Lyrics by Annette Forster, Music by David Budget
©2010 www.budgesongs.co.uk

WHAT YOU'VE GIVEN ME
Music & Lyrics by David Budget ©2010

References and Acknowledgements:

Every effort has been made to identify copyright on the selections within Journey. The author apologise for any instance where copyright has been inadvertently omitted or incorrectly acknowledged.

REFERENCES

Apollinaire, Guillaume, and Roger Shattuck. *Selected Writings of Guillaume Apollinaire.* New York: McGraw-Hill, 1971.
Aristotle, *Introduction to Aristotle.* Edited by Richard McKeon. New York: Modern Library, 1992.
___. *The Complete Works of Aristotle.* Edited by Jonathan Barnes. Princeton: Princeton University, 1984.
Aurelius, Marcus. *The Meditations of Marcus Aurelius.* Edited by George Long. New York: Washington Square, 1993.
Bach, Richard. *Illusions: The Adventures of a Reluctant Messiah.* New York: Delacorte, 1977.
Baird, David. *A Thousand Paths to Enlightenment.* MQ Publications, 2000.
Barron, Frank. *Creative Person and Creative Process.* New York: McGraw-Hill, 1969.
Brown, Pamela. *The Swish of the Curtain.* New York: McGraw-Hill, 2006.

Budget, David. "What You've Given Me." *BudgeSongs*. http://www.budgesongs.co.uk

Caddy, Eileen. *Footprints on the Path*. The Park, Forres, Scotland: Findhorn, 1976.

___. *God Spoke to Me*. The Park, Forres, Scotland. Findhorn, 1971.

Cainer, Jonathan. Jonathan Cainer Official Website : http://www.jonathancainer.com

Collin, Rodney. *The Theory of Celestial Influence – Man, the Universe and Cosmic Mystery*. London: Stuart & Watkins, 1954.

___. *The Theory of Conscious Harmony – From the Letters of Rodney Collin*. London: Vincent Stuart, 1958,

Epictetus. *The Discourses: A Classical Guide to Freedom and Happiness*. Los Osos: B & L Cooper, 1986.

___. *Enchiridion*. Translated by George Long. Amherst: Prometheus Books, 1955.

Ehrmann, Max. "Child of the Universe." ©1927, copyright renewed in 1954 by Bertha K. Ehrmann.

Etheridge, Melissa. "Talking to My Angel." *Yes I Am*. Island Records, 1993.

Exley, Helen. *Words on Courage*. Watford Hertfordshire: Helen Exley Giftbooks, 1998.

Faithfull, Marianne. "The Ballad of Lucy Jordan." Lyrics by Shel Silverstein. Island Records, 1979.

Gibran, Kahlil. *The Prophet*. London: Pan Books, 1991.

Gilbert, Creighton et.al. *Complete Poems and Selected Letters of Michelangelo*. New York: McGraw-Hill, 1980.

Guru R. H. H. *Talk Does not Cook the Rice, Series 2 – A Commentary on the Teaching of Agni Yoga*. York Beach: Foundations of Culture, 1985.

von Goethe, Johann Wolfgang. *Italian Journey*. Translated by W. H. Auden and E. Mayer. New York: Penguin Classics, 1962.

___. *Johann Wolfgang von Goethe*. New York: Penguin, 1992.

___. *Johann Wolfgang von Goethe Selected Poems*. Edited by

Christopher Middleton. Translated by Michael Hamburger. London: J. Caldur, 1988.

___. *Conversations with Goethe*. London: J. M. Dent & Sons, 1935.

Hayward, Susan. *Begin it Now*. Australia: In Tune Books, 1987.

___. *Being, Reminders from the Gods*. Australia: In Tune Books, 1997.

Henley, Don. "For My Wedding." *The Very Best of Don Henley*. Words by Larry John McNally. Geffen, 2009.

Leoni. E. *Nostradamus and His Prophecies*. New York: Wing Books, 2000.

Mandela, Nelson. *Long Walk to Freedom: The Autobiography of Nelson Mandela*. Boston: Little Brown, 1994.

McDowell, Josh, and Bill Wilson. *Christianity, A Ready Defence*. San Bernandino: Here's Life, 1990.

Montaigne, Michael. *Complete Essays of Montaigne by M.E. De Montaigne*. Palo Alto: Stanford University, 1958.

Ouspensky, P. D. *Conscience, The Search for Truth*. London: Arkana, 1988.

___. *The Cosmology of Man's Possible Evolution*. East Sussix: Agora Books, 1989.

___. *The Fourth Way – A Record of Talks and Answers to Questions based on the Teaching of G. I. Gurdjieff*. London: Routledge & Kegan Paul, 1957.

___. *The Psychology of Man's Possible Evolution*. New York: Knopf, 1945.

Phillips, Michael, and Salli Rasberry. *Honest Business*. New York: Random House, 1981.

Plato. *Complete Works by Plato*. Editor John M. Cooper and D. S. Hutchinson. Indianapolis: Hackett Pub Co, 1997.

Ramtha. Edited by Steven Lee Weinberg PhD, from *Ramtha Dialogues*, tape recordings channeled by J.Z. Knight of Yelm, Washington State. First published in 1986 by Sovereignty Inc, Box 1865, Bellevue, WA 98009, USA.

Rilke, Rainer, Maria. *Ahead of All Parting: The Selected Poetry and Prose of Rainier Maria Rilke.* Edited and Translated by Setphen Mitchell. New York : Modern Library, 1995.

_ _ _ . *Letters to a Young Poet.* Translated by M. D. Herter. New York: W. W. Norton & Company, Inc. 1954.

_ _ _ . *The Selected Poetry of Rainer Maria Rilke.* Edited by Stephen Mitchell.New York: McGraw-Hill, 1989.

Schiller, Friedrich. *The Aesthetic Letters, Essays, and the Philosophical Letters of Schiller; Tr.* New York: McGraw-Hill, 2010.

Stengel, Richard. "Nelson Mandela's Eight Rules of Leadership," *Time Magazine*, 2008. July 9, 2008, www.time.com

Shakespeare, William. *The Complete Works of William Shakespeare.* New York: McGraw-Hill, 1990.

The Holy Bible, King James Version *References of Angels used: Acts 12:6-15, Psalm 103:20-21, Isaiah 37:36, Matthew 18:10-14, Psalm 91:11-16, 1 Peter 3:22, Colossians 2:18, 2 Corinthians 11:14, Rev 22:8-9, Luke 22:43, Job 33:23-26, Daniel 10:13, Hebrews 1:14, Revelation 5:11-12*

Train. "Drops of Jupiter." Songwriters: Charlie Colin, Robert S. Hotchkiss, Pat Monahan, James W. Stafford and Scott Michael Underwood. *Drops of Jupiter*. Columbia Records, 2001.

Tredennick, Hugh, and Robin Waterfield. *Conversations of Socrates.* New York: McGraw-Hill, 1990.

Waters, Rogers. "The Tide is Turning." *Radio K.A.O.S.* Columbia Records, 1987.

Whitman, Walt. *Leaves of Grass.* London: Signet Classics, 1980.

Wikipedia. "Faith." http://en.wikipedia.org/wiki/Faith.

Zapiro. *Zapiro's Official Website.* http://www.zapiro.com

About the Author

South African born Annette Forster is a true daughter of the universe. Born in 1969 in South Africa during the era of apartheid, Annette lived through the struggle and emergence of the Rainbow nation. Although lambasted with angry rhetoric and surrounded by a volatile society of racial tensions, she developed a sense of equality, justice and harmony as she experienced the rebirth of South Africa. Through it all, she kept her sunshine smile.

Annette has a natural thirst for knowledge and personal growth, and her pursuit of knowledge is reflected in her academic achievements. She has earned two Bachelor of Commerce degrees and a Master of Business Administration (MBA) with distinction.

Annette has travelled extensively and pursued an International Business career. Her talent in business allowed her to pursue her personal quest to travel, discover her own philosophy of "home" and improve her understanding of diverse cultures and philosophies. She is a mother of two (whom she describes as her greatest achievements) and the vast range of experiences that she sought out, only served to further influence Annette's true passion: writing. She is an exciting new author and poet.

www.annetteforster.info

Lightning Source UK Ltd.
Milton Keynes UK
26 March 2011

169883UK00001B/57/P

9 781452 079233